Popular Songs For Classical/ Fingerstyle Guitar:

21 Intermediate Arrangements.

Notation and Tab Edition

By Adrian Allan

Edited by Allan H. Jones

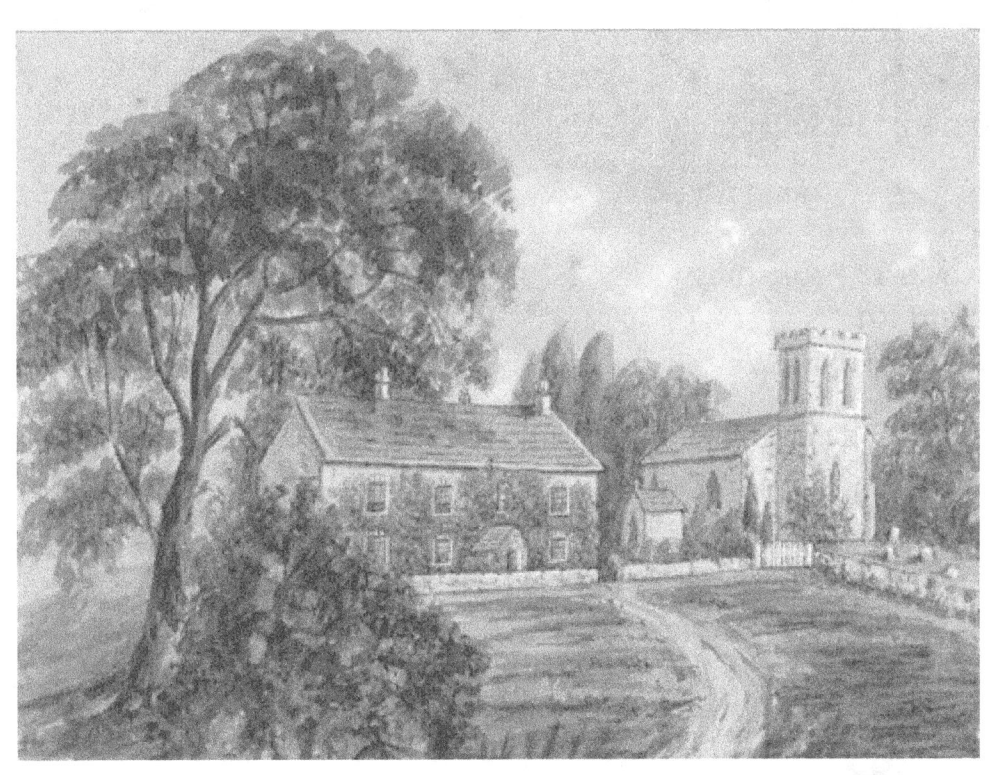

Meadow Music Publishing

First Edition: 2018

ISBN: 978-0-244-99437-2

Meadow Music Publishing
23c Burford Rd
Manchester, M16 8EW

adrianallan12345@gmail.com

www.facebook.com/meadowmusicpublishing/

Front cover: anonymous Victorian watercolour

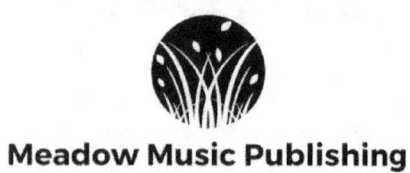

Meadow Music Publishing

Contents

Preface   v

Background Information on the Music

Stephen Foster Songs   v

Folk Songs   vi

Parlour Songs   vii

Classical Arrangements   viii

Stephen Foster Songs

My Old Kentucky Home   2

Beautiful Dreamer   4

Jeanie With The Light Brown Hair   6

Hard Times Come Again No More   8

Gentle Annie   10

Reproduction of Sheet Music for Beautiful Dreamer, 1864   12

Folk Songs

Allan Water   14

The Lark In The Clear Air   15

David Of The White Rock   16

Believe Me, If All Those Endearing Young Charms   17

The Skye Boat Song   18

Annie Laurie   19

Deep River   20

Images of the Irish Tenor, John McCormack   22

Parlour Songs

At Dawning   24

I Love You Truly   25

Kiss Me Again   26

My Wild Irish Rose   28

Love's Old Sweet Song   30

Reproduction of Sheet Music for Love's Old Sweet Song, 1884   32

Classical Arrangements

Chanson De Matin by Edward Elgar   34

I Vow To Thee My Country by Gustav Holst   36

Waltz From Coppelia by Leo Delibes   38

Waltz From Swan Lake by Pytor Tchaikovsky   40

Other Books Available   42

Preface

Intermediate players are often in search of a wide variety of pieces in order to expand their repertoire. The pieces in the volume are varied, and serve as a departure from the Spanish repertoire with which the guitar is so often associated. The easiest pieces to approach are the folk songs, which are short and simple in structure. The songs by Foster are perhaps a little more challenging. In contrast, the classical pieces contain more unusual voicings and often require playing in the higher positions. Parlour songs represent something between; they are part of a musical tradition that is fundamentally melodic, but tend to borrow chromatic chords from the classical tradition. For higher-level players (grades 7 and above), all the pieces offer excellent sight-reading material, or a change from the rigours of the advanced guitar repertoire.

Background Information on the Music

Stephen Foster Songs

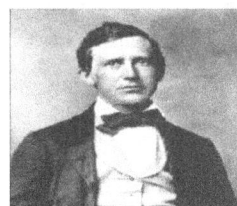 Stephen Foster (1826-1864) is often credited as "America's First Composer". Foster's songs are American in character, revolving around the themes of home, rivers, the Civil War and life on the plantation. In 1860 he moved to New York City. Foster left a legacy of over 200 songs, many of which are still popular today.

My Old Kentucky Home is an anti-slavery ballad that was probably composed in 1852. The song describes the life of a plantation slave and the hardships that are endured, "A few more days for to tote the weary load, no matter, 'twill never be light".

Beautiful Dreamer was published in 1864, as the original sheet music suggests, it was his last song: "Composed but a few days prior to his death". The song tells of a lover serenading a "beautiful dreamer". The song is in the time signature of 9/8, which is a rare occurrence in songwriting.

Jeanie With The Light Brown Hair was published in 1854. It was possibly composed as an attempt at reconciliation with his estranged wife, "Jenny". The verses start with the phrases, "I dreamed of", "I long for", "I sigh for".

Hard Time Come Again No More was published in 1854. The song asks the listener to consider the plight of the less fortunate. It begins with the lines, "Let us pause in life's pleasures and count its many tears". This arrangement uses an "alberti-bass" which features in the original piano score.

Gentle Annie was composed in 1856. There is some dispute over which Annie the song refers to; it could have been Foster's friend, his aunt, or his maternal grandmother. The opening melody bears more than a passing resemblance to *Annie Laurie*, which was a very popular song among Scottish and Irish soldiers before and during the American Civil War.

Parlour Songs

Parlour songs take their name from the parlours in middle-class homes where music was performed by family and friends at the piano. They reached their heyday in the late nineteenth to early twentieth century, and were disseminated in the form of sheet music (before the invention of the phonograph). Parlour songs feature the late Victorian/ Edwardian themes of domesticity, the countryside and nostalgia.

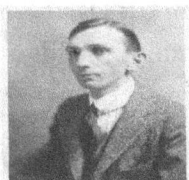

At Dawning by Charles Wakefield Cadman was written in collaboration with the lyricist Nelle Richmond Eberhart. It encapsulates themes of love and nature: "When the dawn flames in the sky, I love you. When the birdlings wake and cry, I love you".

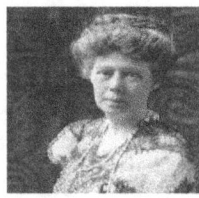

I Love You Truly was composed by the American songwriter Carrie Jacobs Bond in 1901. It sold over a million copies and recorded by many famous vocalists, such as Bing Crosby and Nelson Eddy. This arrangement features a dropped-D tuning.

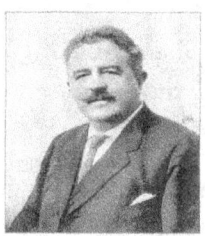

Kiss Me Again was written by Victor August Herbert (1859 – 1924). He was an Irish-born, German-raised American composer, cellist and conductor. Although Herbert enjoyed important careers as a cello soloist and conductor, he is best known for composing many successful operettas that premiered on Broadway from the 1890s to World War I. Kiss Me Again is taken from the operetta *Millie Modiste* (1905).

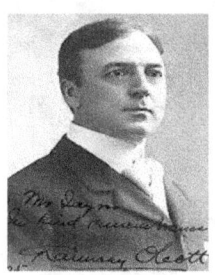

My Wild Irish Rose was written by the Irish-American Chauncey Olcott in 1899. The inspiration for the song was revealed by his wife Margaret after his death. On a visit to his mother's homeland in 1898, a young boy gave her a flower. When she asked him what it was called he replied "...a wild Irish Rose." The song enjoyed renewed popularity after a 1947 film was released about the life of the composer.

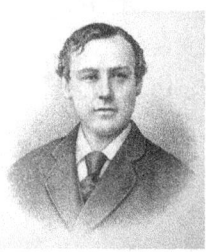

Love's Old Sweet Song was published in 1884 by the Irish composer James Lynam Molloy and lyricist G. Clifton Bingham. It features a lengthy verse in a different time signature to the chorus, which is an unusual feature. It was one of the most popular songs of the late-Victorian to Edwardian period.

Folk Songs

Folk songs are often described as songs that have been passed down through an orally-transmitted tradition, but the reality is often more nuanced. Sometimes we know the name of the composer, and on other occasions, they were printed as broadsides, later to be compiled and collected by folklorists. Their authenticity is further compromised by arrangers and editors who alter both their lyrical and melodic content. Even though "true" folk songs are hard to pin down, we have rich repertoire of songs to choose from, many of which are ideally suited to the guitar.

Allan Water was composed by Matthew ("Monk") Lewis (1775-1818). It is a charming piece about a Scottish river in central Scotland. Rising in the Ochil Hills, it runs through Strathallan to Dunblane and Bridge of Allan before joining the River Forth.

The Lark In The Clear Air was written by Samuel Ferguson in the eighteenth century. It has always been a favourite of the Irish repertoire ever since. It was later arranged by Ralph Vaughan Williams. Take care while playing the triplets in the melody.

David Of The White Rock was probably composed by David Owen (1712–1741), a harpist and composer who lived near Porthmadog in Caernarfonshire. He was known locally as *Dafydd y Garreg Wen* ("David of the White Rock"). The words were written over 100 years later by the poet John Ceiriog Hughes (1832–1887). The arrangement here has a chorale-type texture, where most beats of the bar are harmonised on a different chord.

Believe Me, If All Those Endearing Young Charms is another favourite Irish folk song was written in 1808 by Irish poet Thomas Moore using a traditional Irish air. It is thought to have been written by Moore to reassure his wife who was suffering from smallpox. This version makes frequent use of the chromatic chord of E diminished seventh. The most famous version of this song was recorded by the great Irish tenor John McCormack, and can be easily accessed on *Youtube*.

The Skye Boat Song is another "folk" song that is not as old as might be imagined. The lyrics were written to an air collected in the 1870s. The song was first published in the popular volume *Songs of the North*. In this arrangement, the fifth string is re-tuned to low G, and the sixth string, to low D.

Annie Laurie is a Scottish song based on a poem said to have been written by William Douglas of Dumfries and Galloway, about his romance with Annie Laurie (1682—1764). The words were modified and the tune was added by Alicia Scott in 1834/5. The tune is also known as "Maxwelton Braes".

Deep River is an anonymous song of African-American origin. It was first seen in print in 1876, and has become one of the best-loved spirituals. It was famously sung by Paul Robeson and was included in the 1929 film, *Show Boat*.

Classical Arrangements

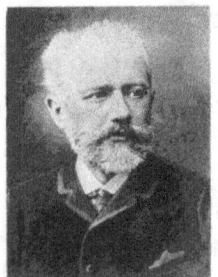

Waltz From Swan Lake by Pyotr Ilyich Tchaikovsky (1840-1893) is taken from the famous ballet composed between 1875-6. Tchaikovsky's other works include symphonies, concertos, operas, ballets, and chamber music. This arrangement offers some challenges; the theme moves up an octave and there are some stretches and barres to negotiate. The melody in the higher octave sounds more expressive when some vibrato is added by the left hand

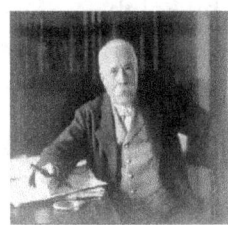

Chanson de Matin (Morning Song) by Edward Elgar (1857-1934) was originally for violin and piano, but later orchestrated by the composer. Its first publication was in 1899. The orchestral version of the work was published two years later, and first performed in 1901. Much of the piece is scored here in three voices – in-between the melody and the bass, a syncopated inner-part fills in the harmony.

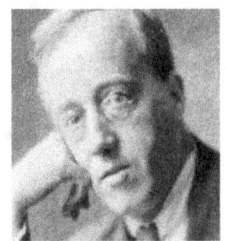

I Vow To Thee My Country is from *The Planets*, a seven-movement orchestral suite by the English composer Gustav Holst (1874-1934), written between 1914 and 1916. Each movement is named after a planet in the Solar System; this one being Jupiter. This grand theme that ends the suite was set by Holst to a patriotic poem by the diplomat Cecil Spring Rice. The arrangement in this book uses a dropped-D tuning. It is perhaps one of the more challenging pieces, as the bass line is prominent and the bass notes need to be given their full value.

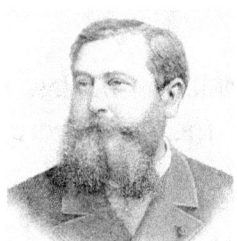

Waltz From Coppelia is by the French composer Leo Delibes (1836 -1891). His music is light, graceful and elegant and is said to reflect the spirit of the Second Empire in France. This arrangement should be played with that spirit in mind; apart from one move up to the seventh position, it adapts to the guitar with relative ease

Stephen Foster Songs

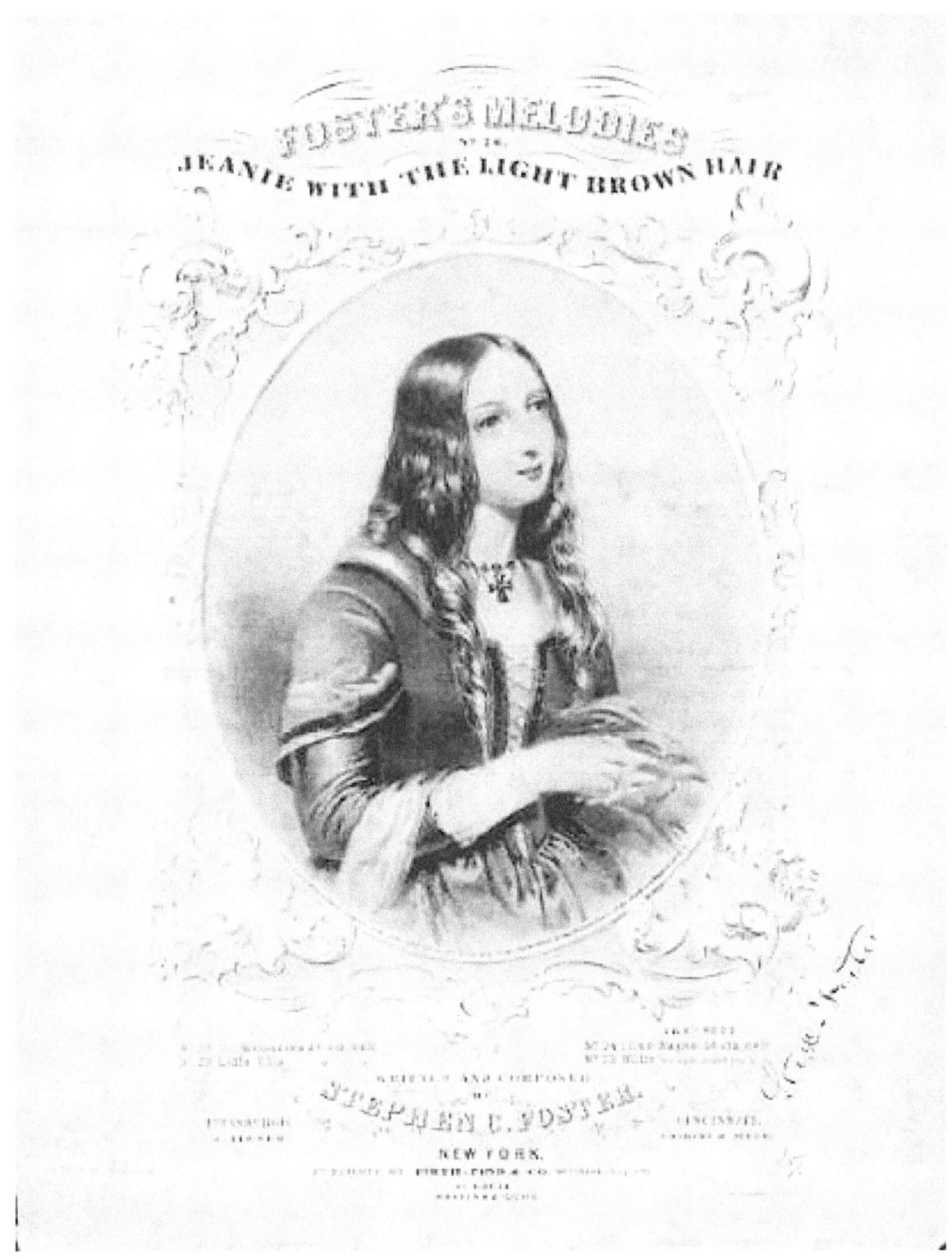

My Old Kentucky Home

Stephen C. Foster

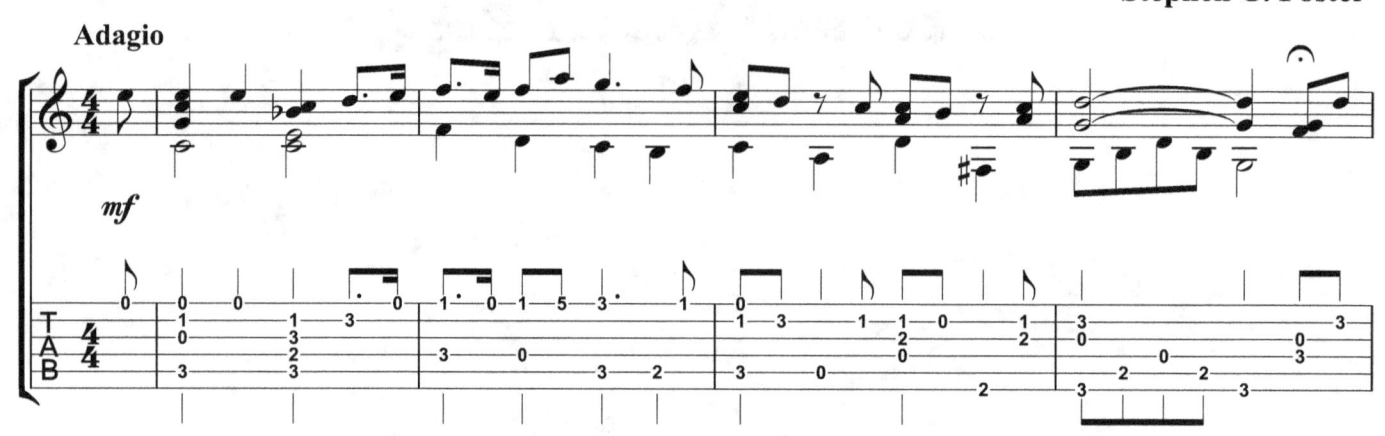

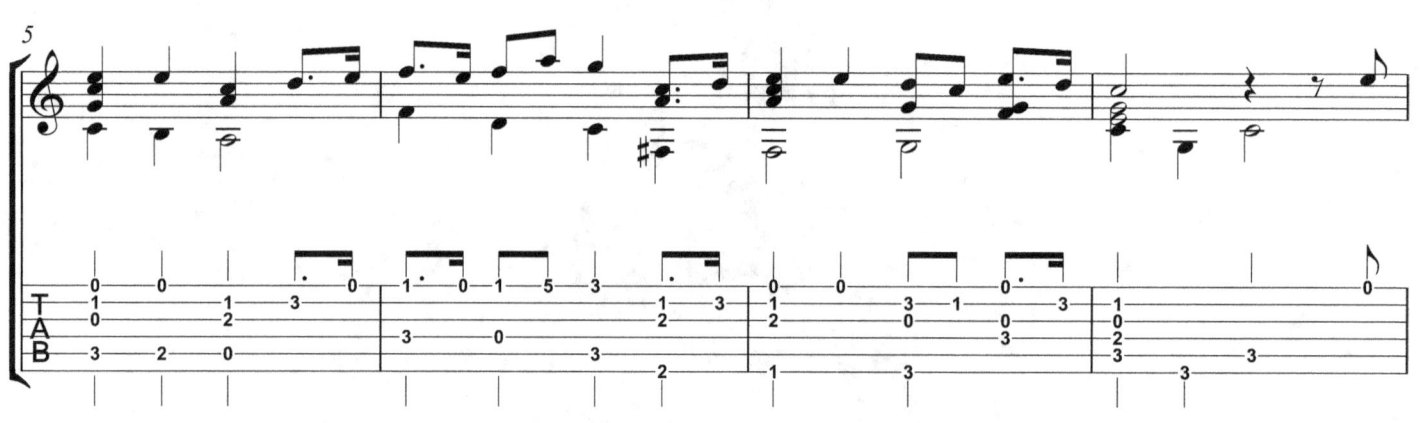

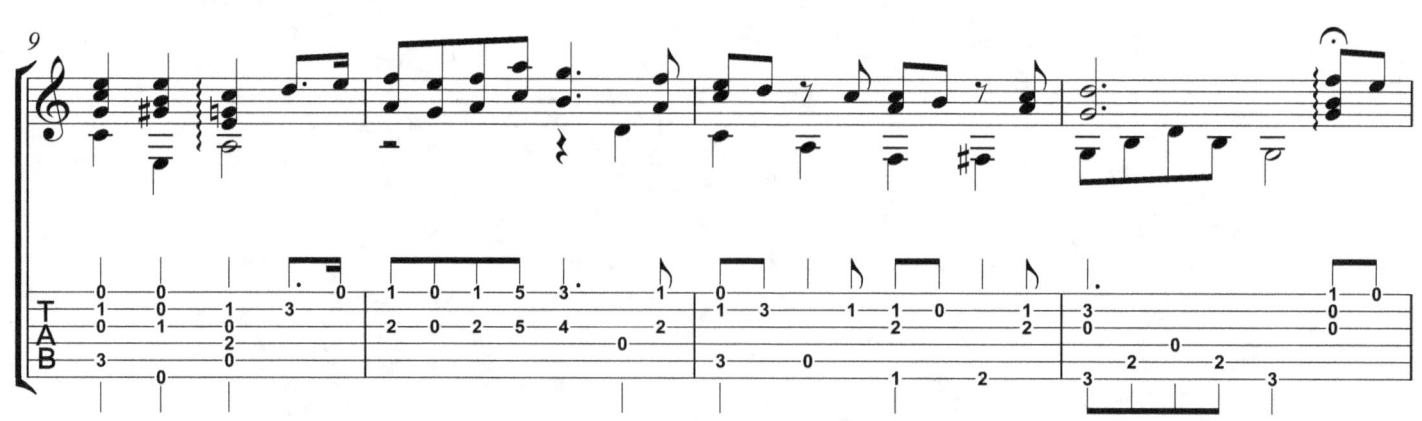

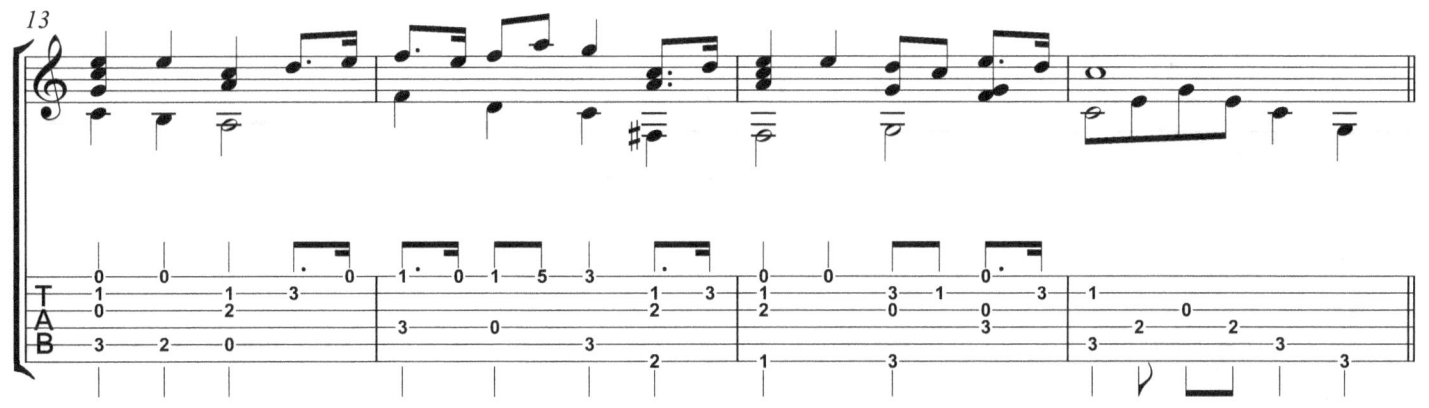

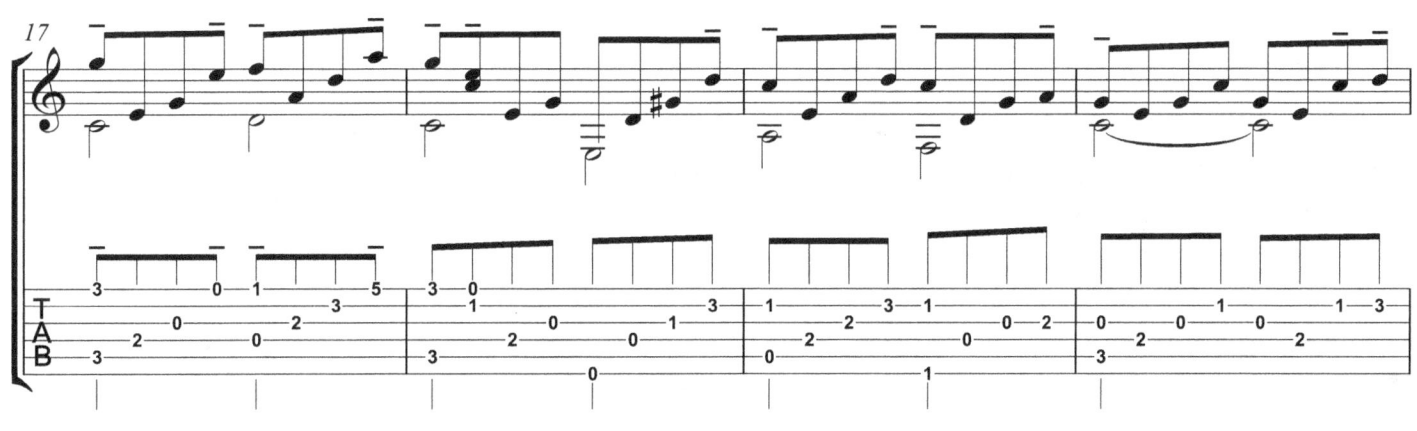

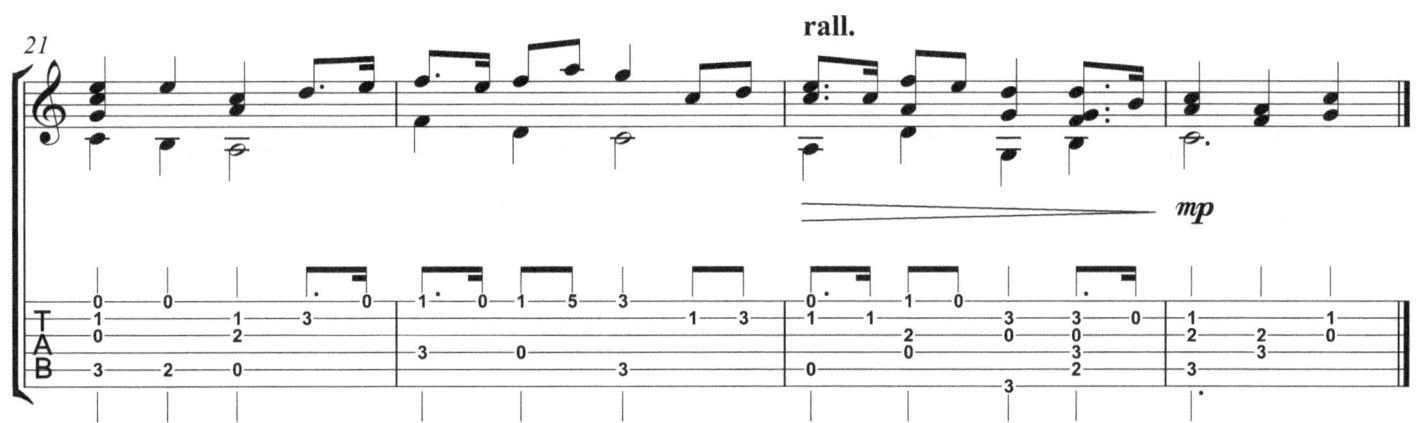

Beautiful Dreamer

Stephen C. Foster

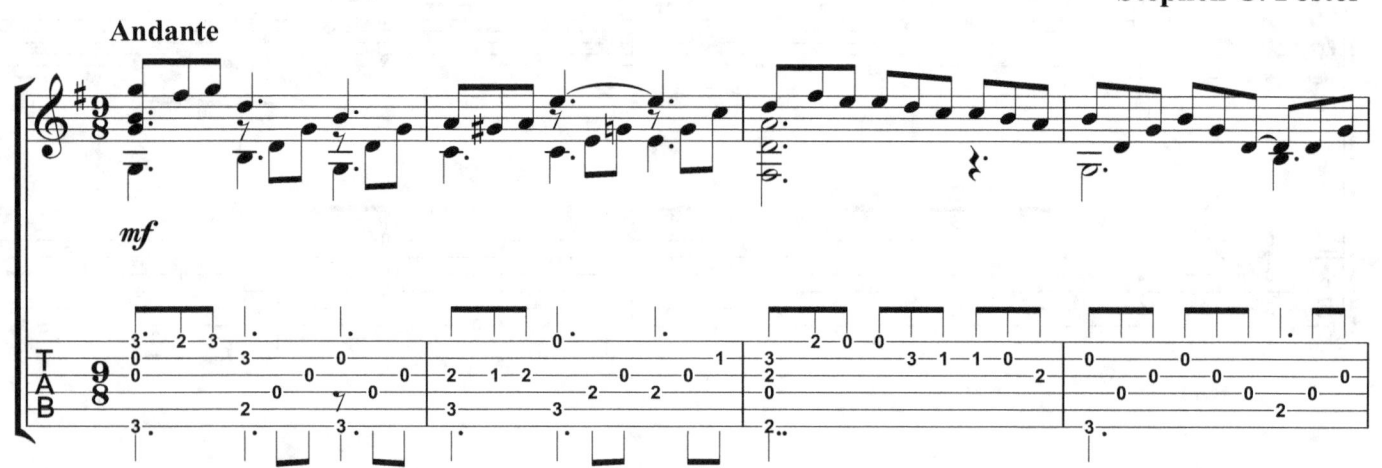

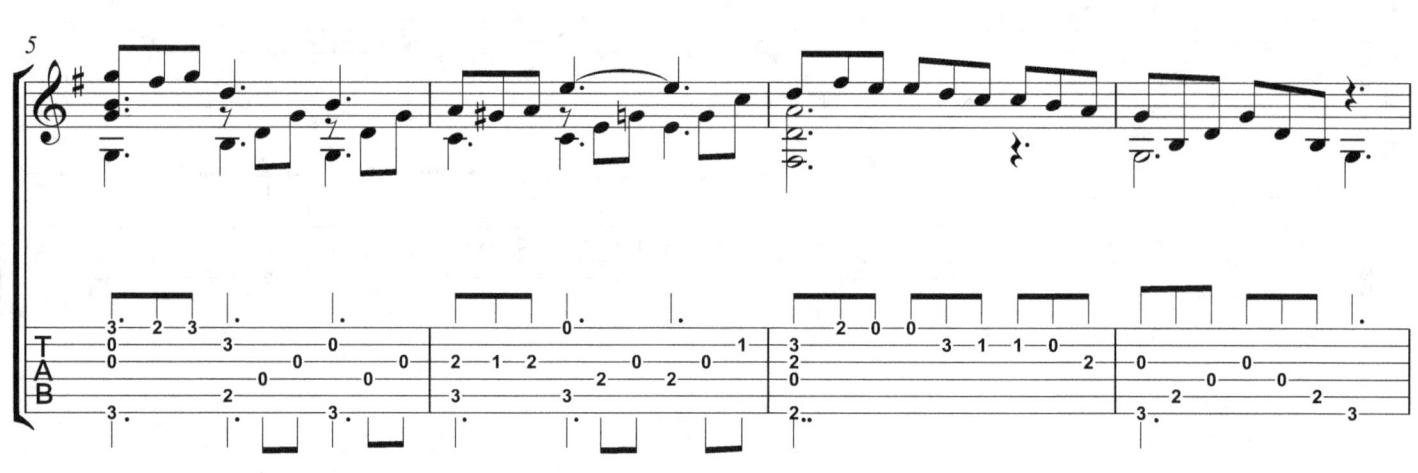

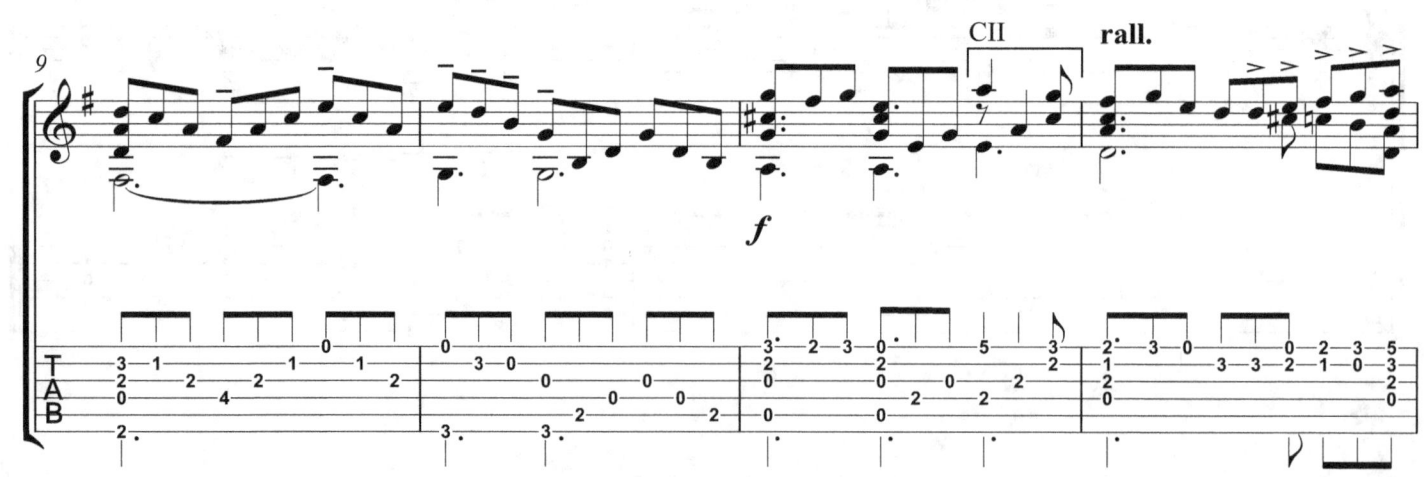

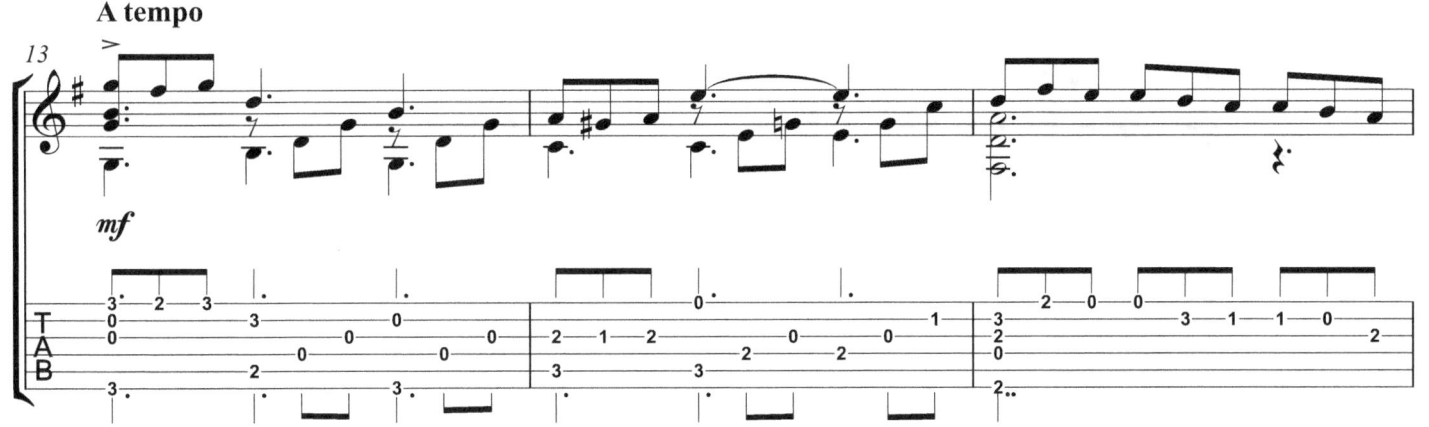

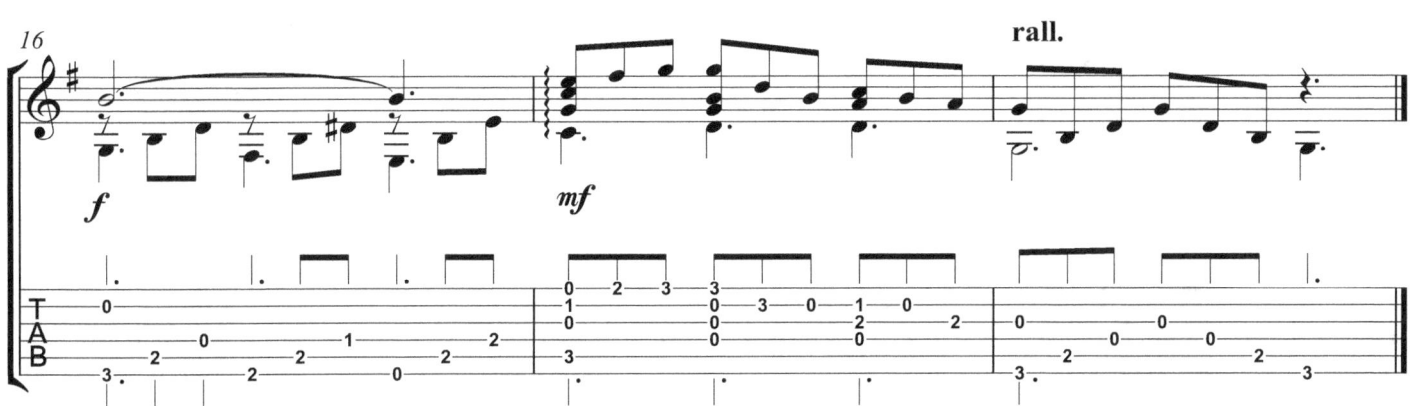

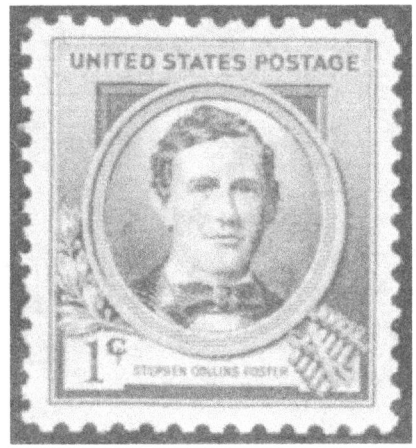

Stephen Foster US postage stamp, 1940

Jeanie With The Light Brown Hair

Stephen C. Foster

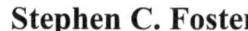

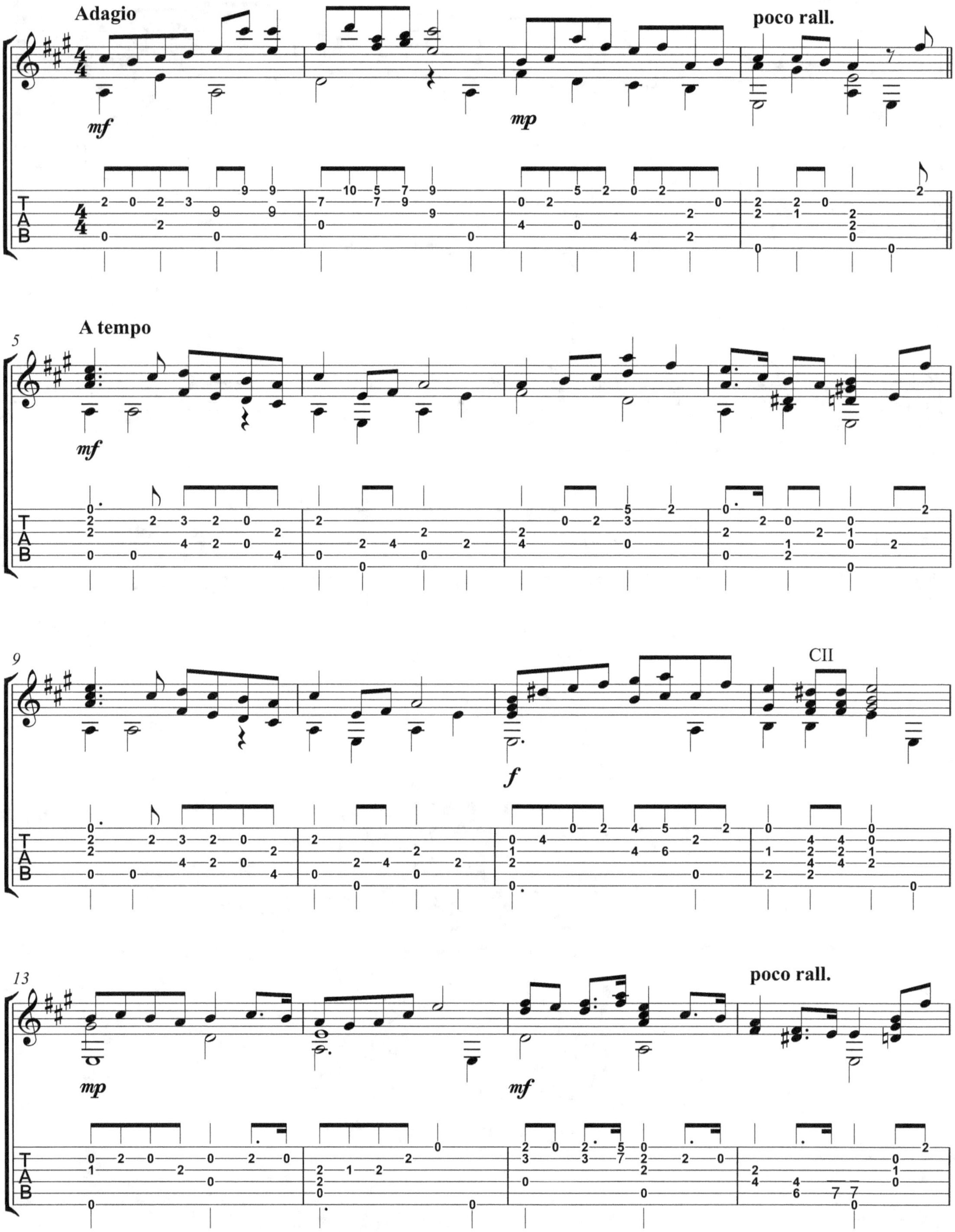

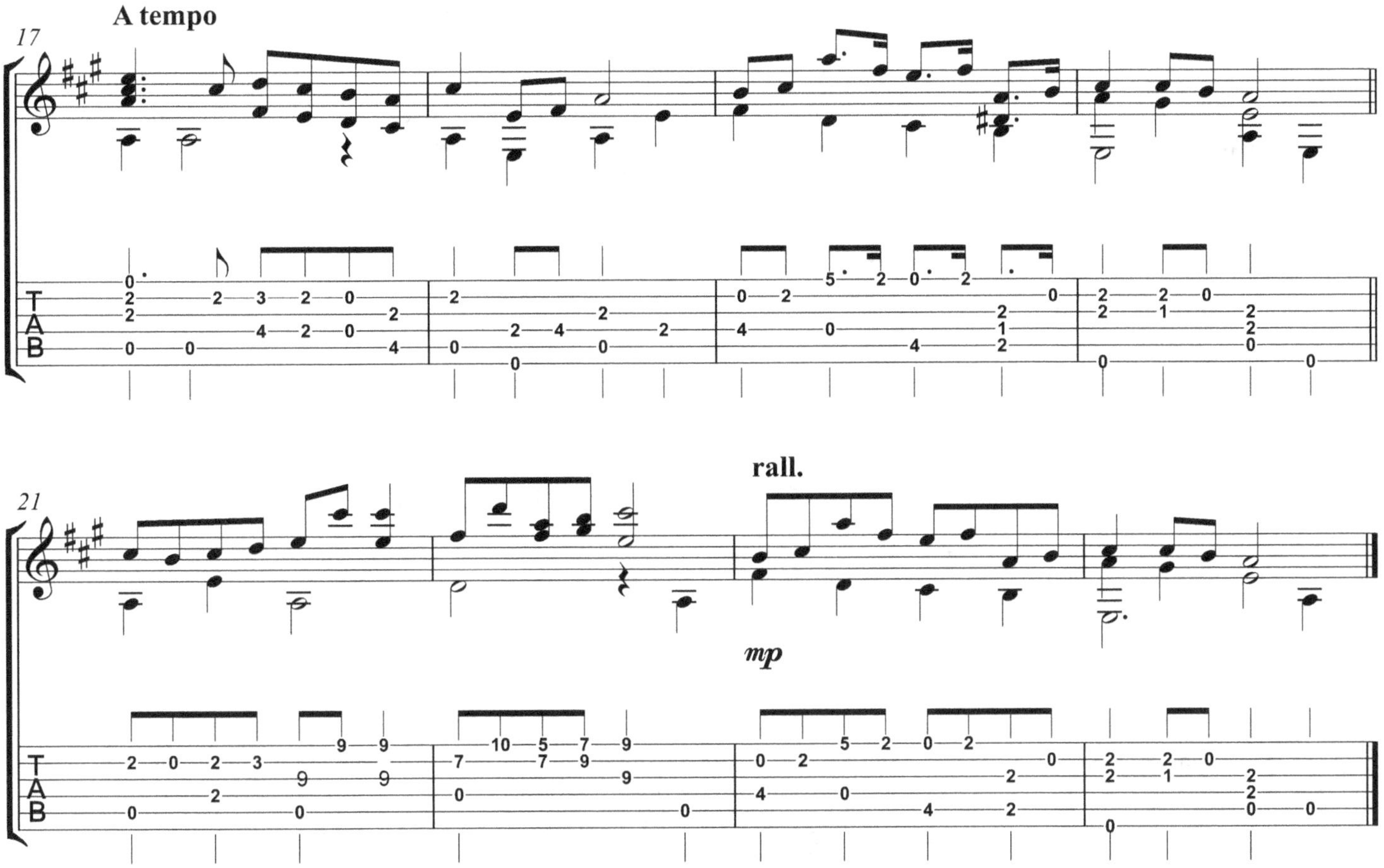

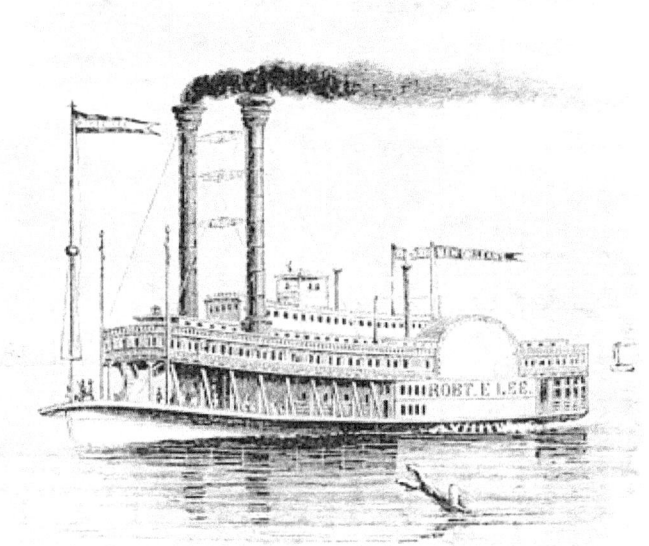

Hard Times Come Again No More

Stephen C. Foster

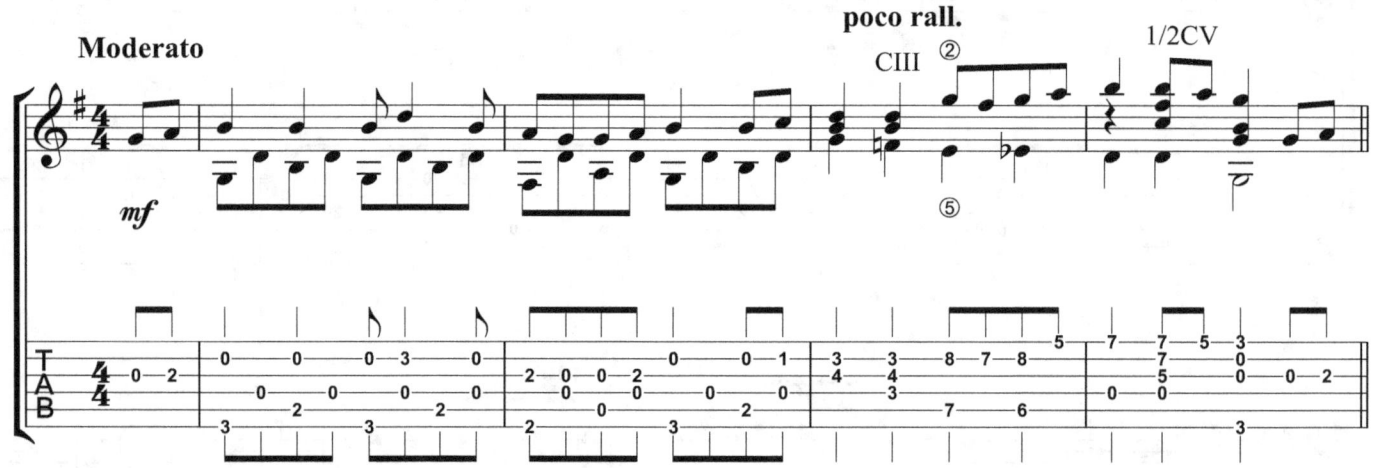

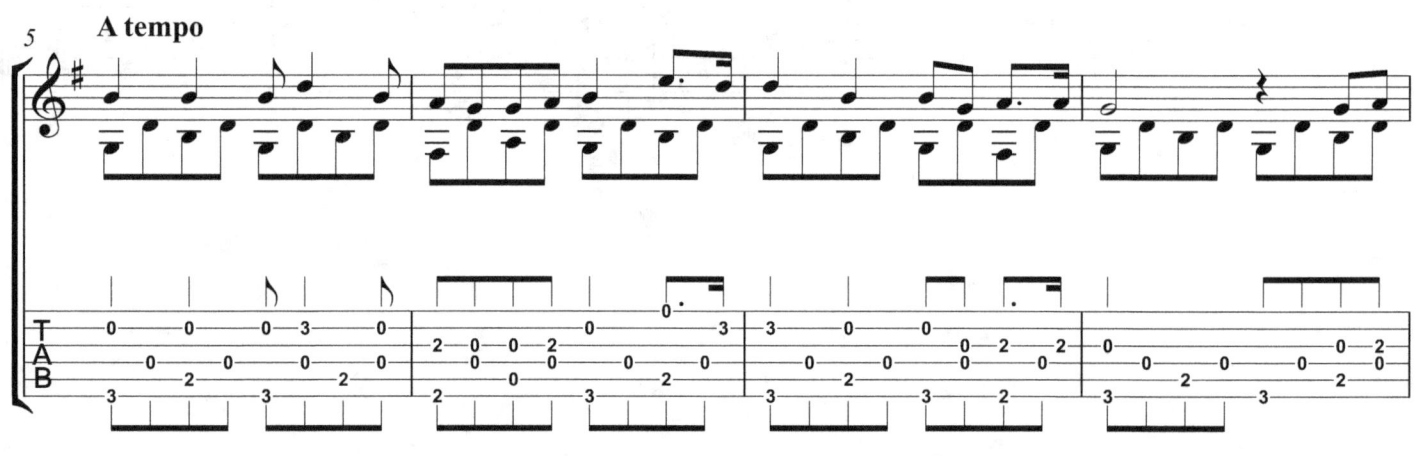

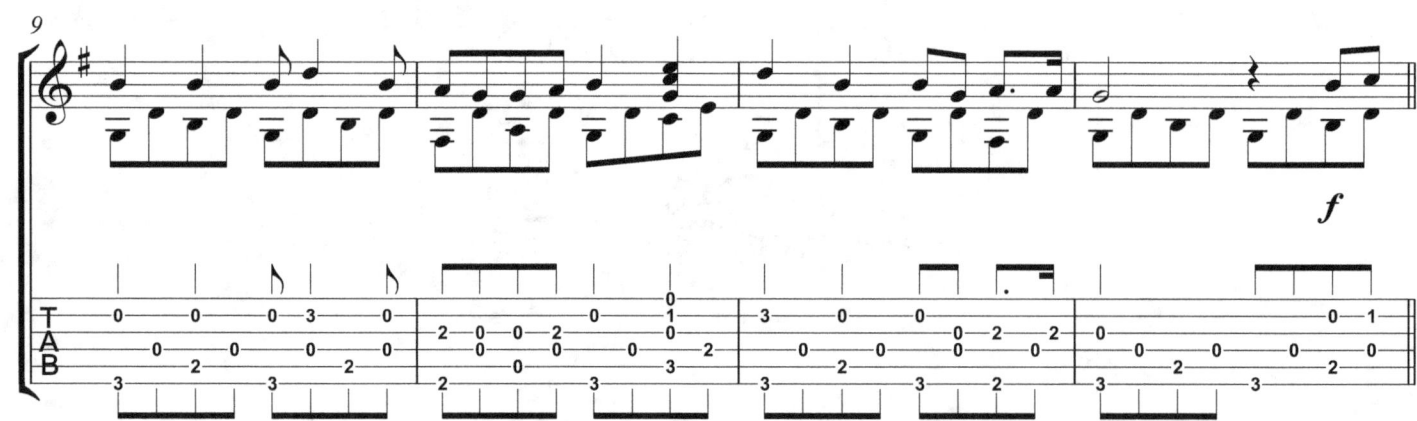

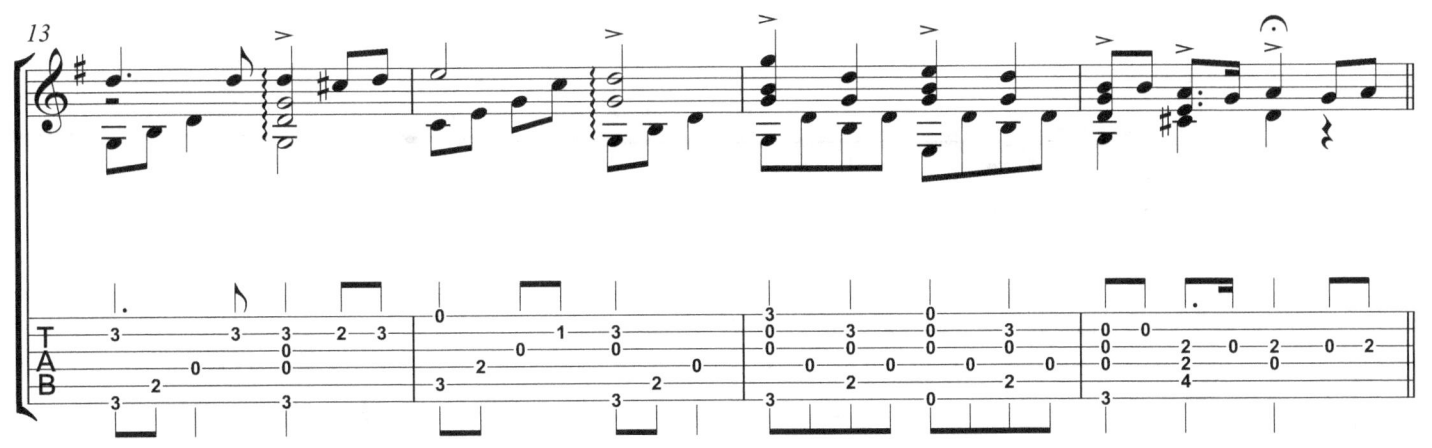

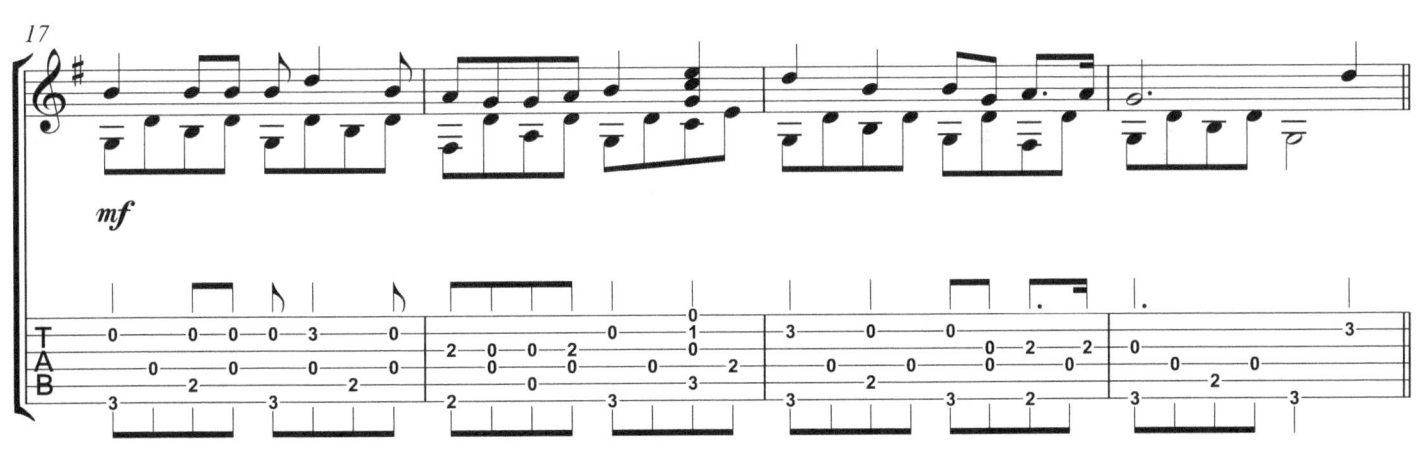

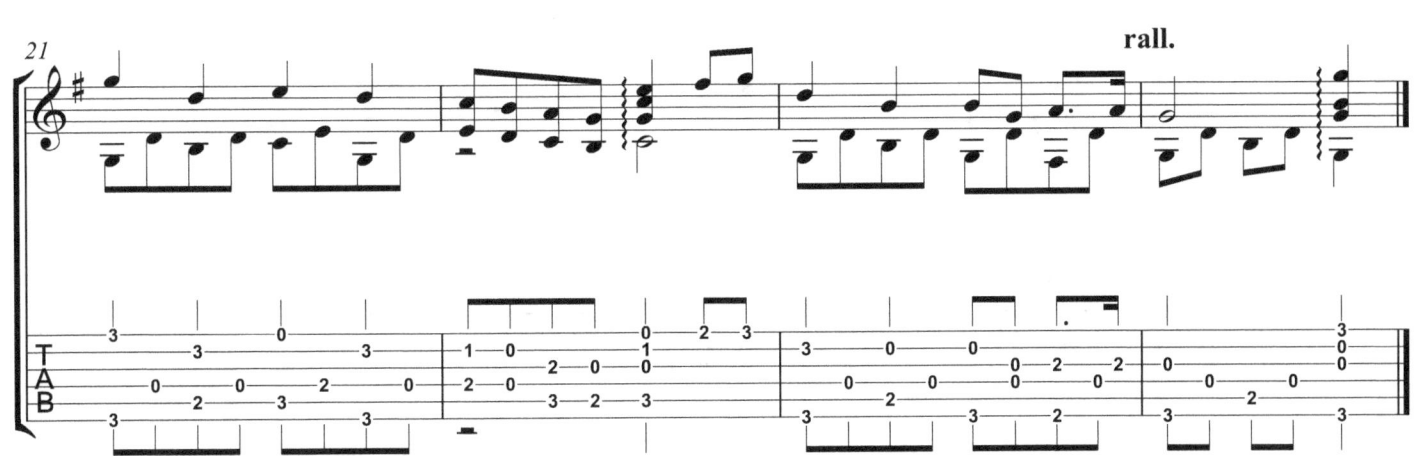

Gentle Annie

Stephen C. Foster

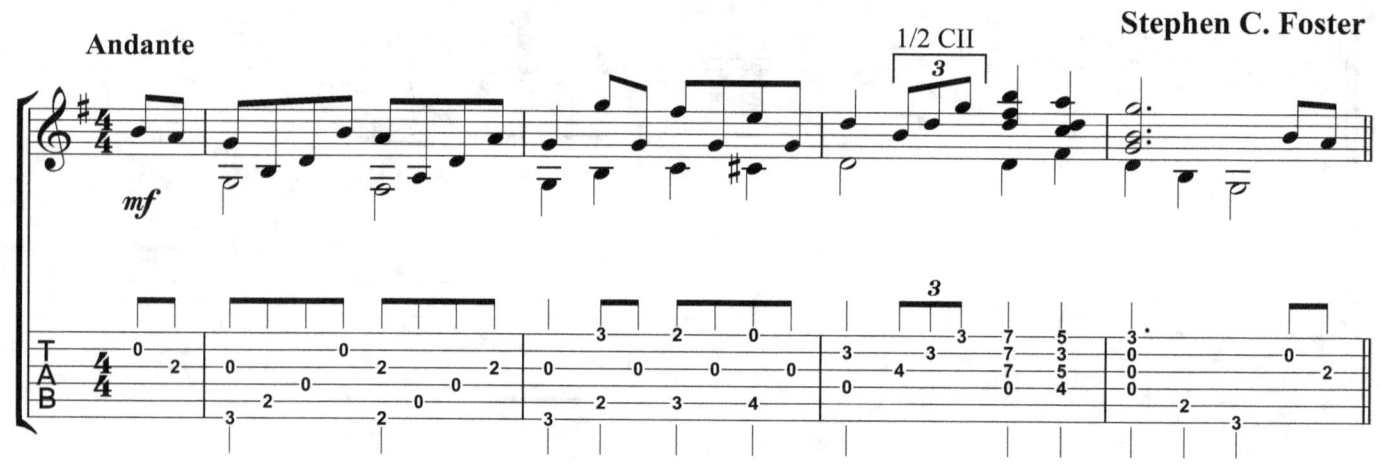

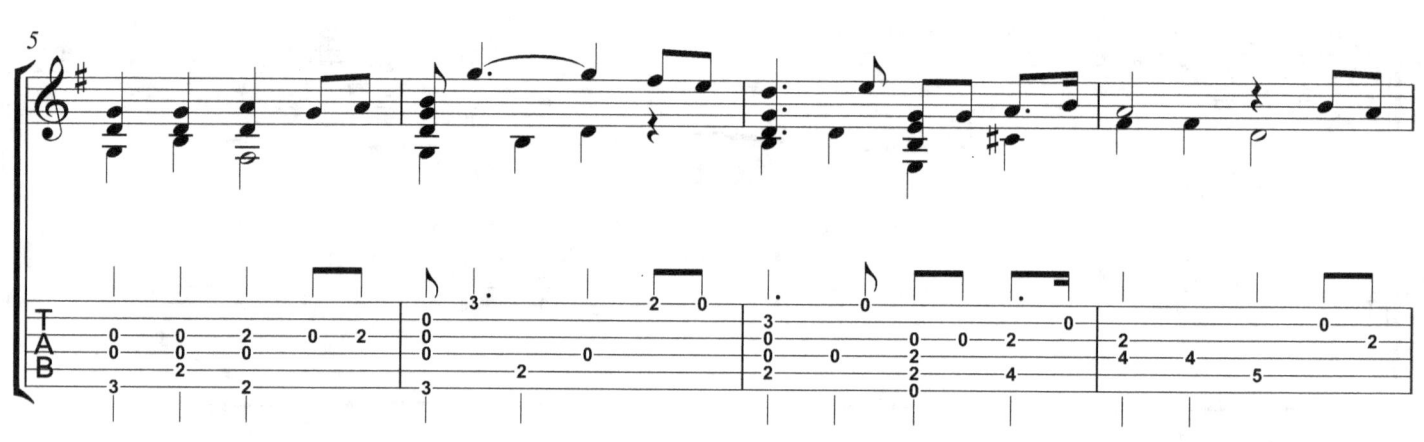

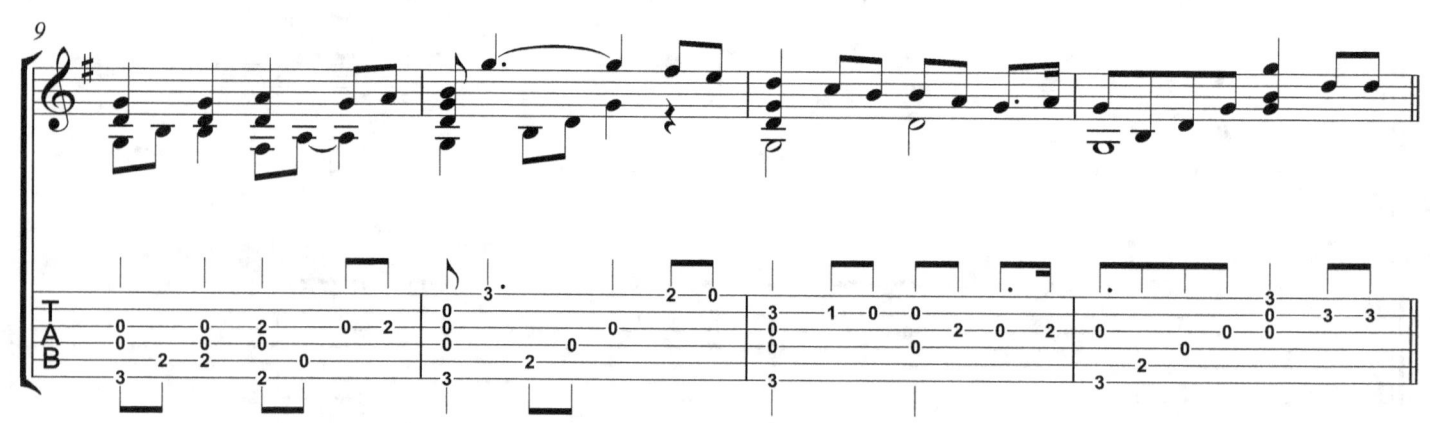

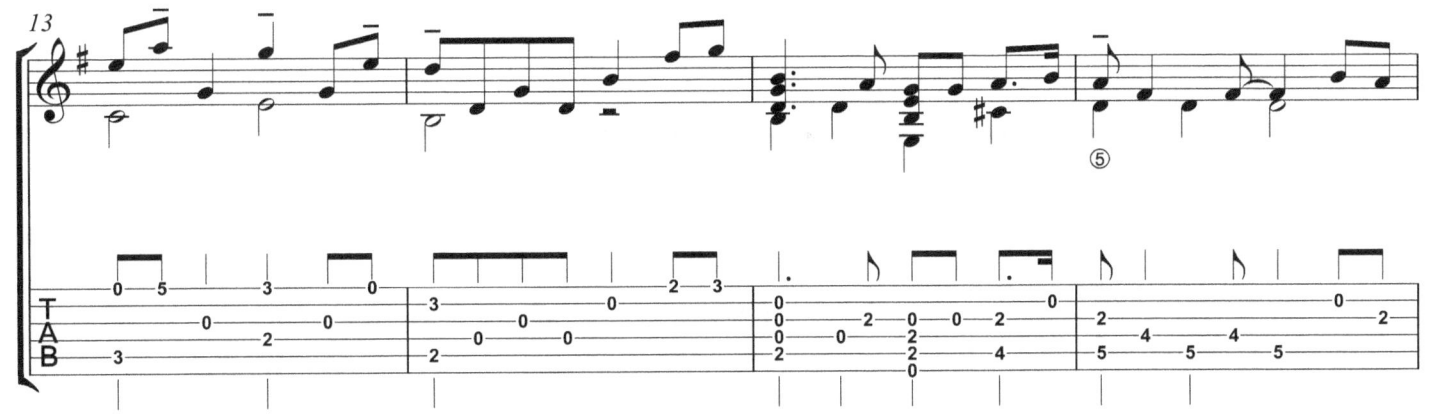

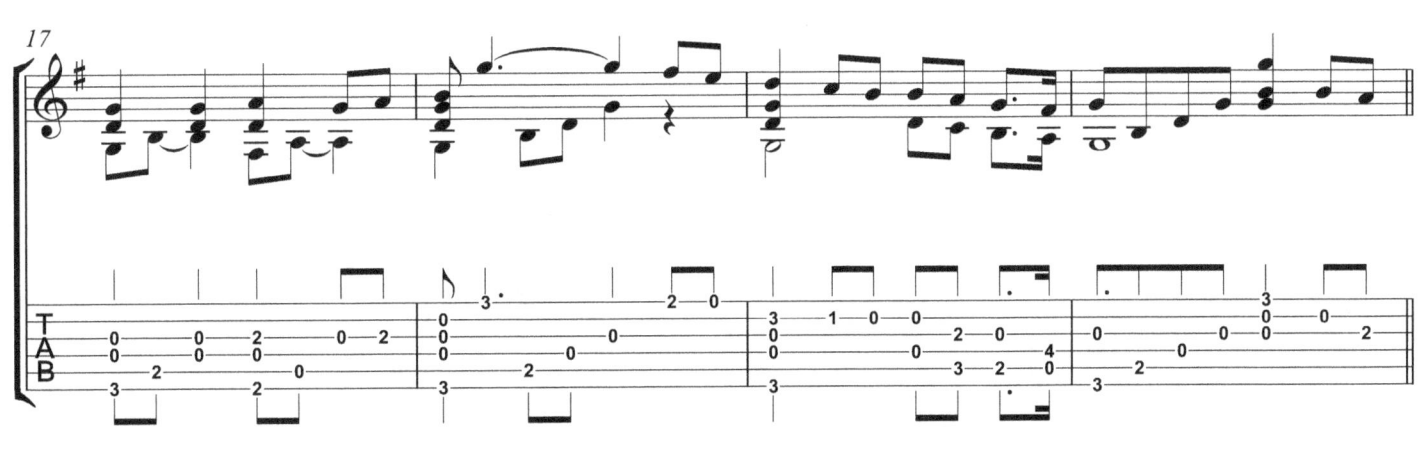

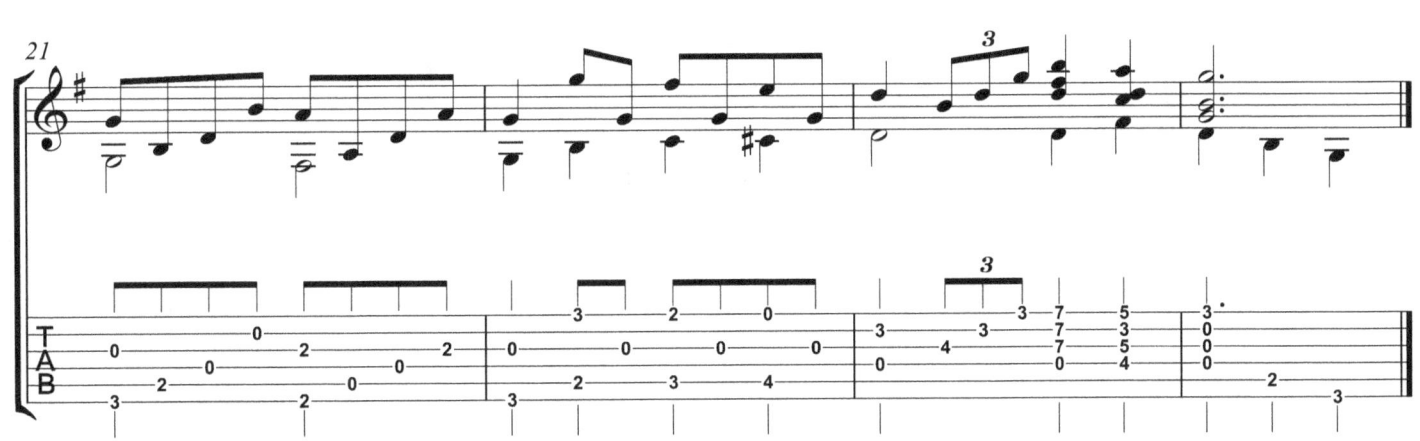

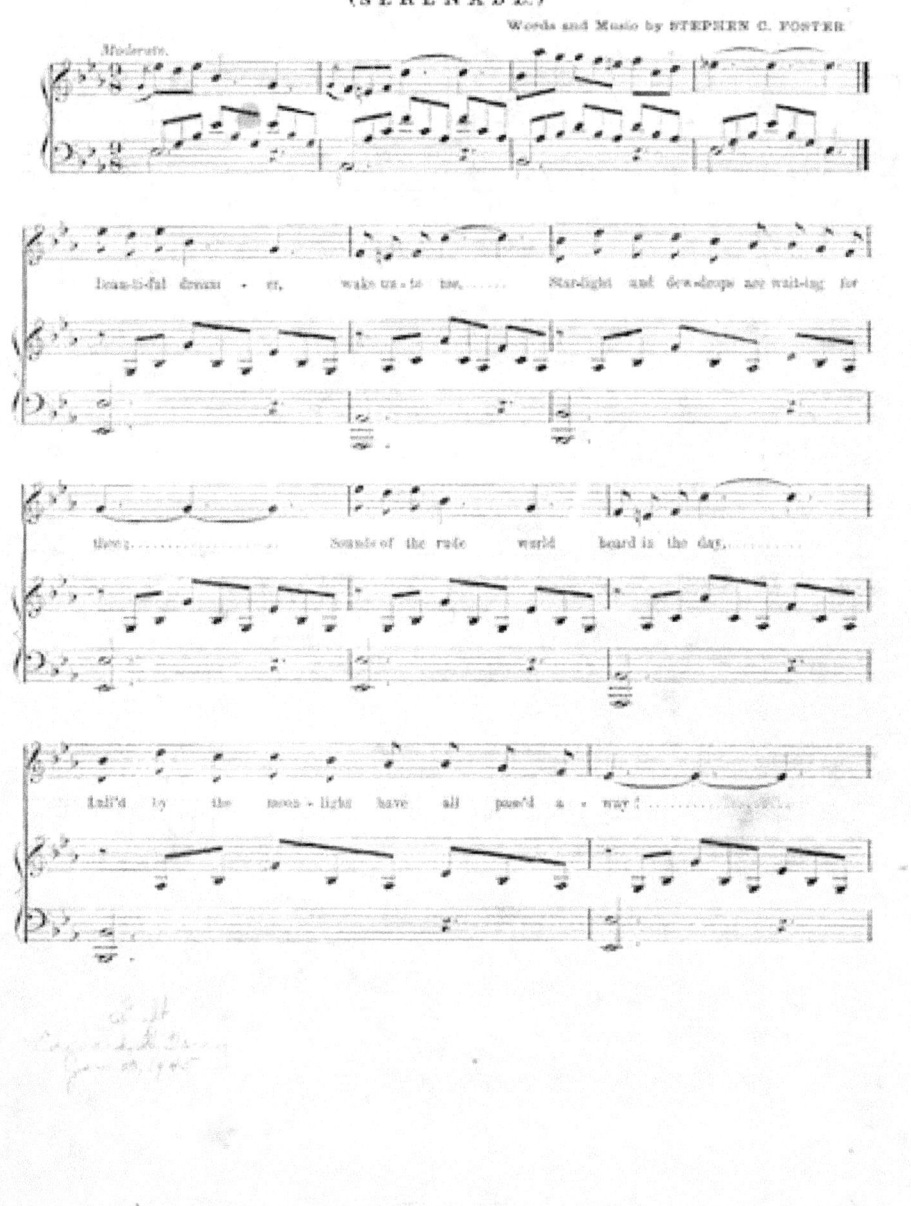

Original Sheet Music For Beautiful Dreamer (1864)

Folk Songs

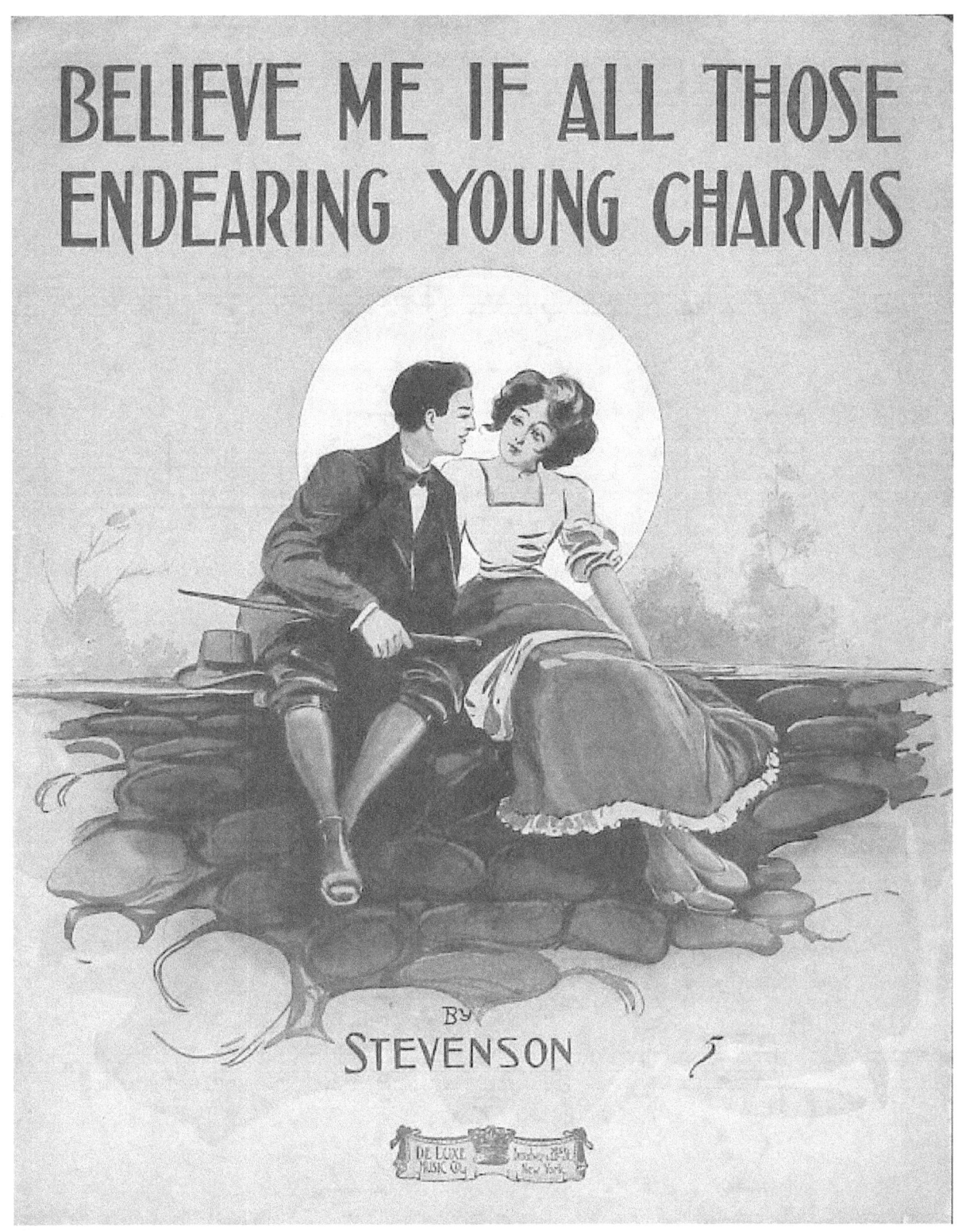

Allan Water

Monk Lewis

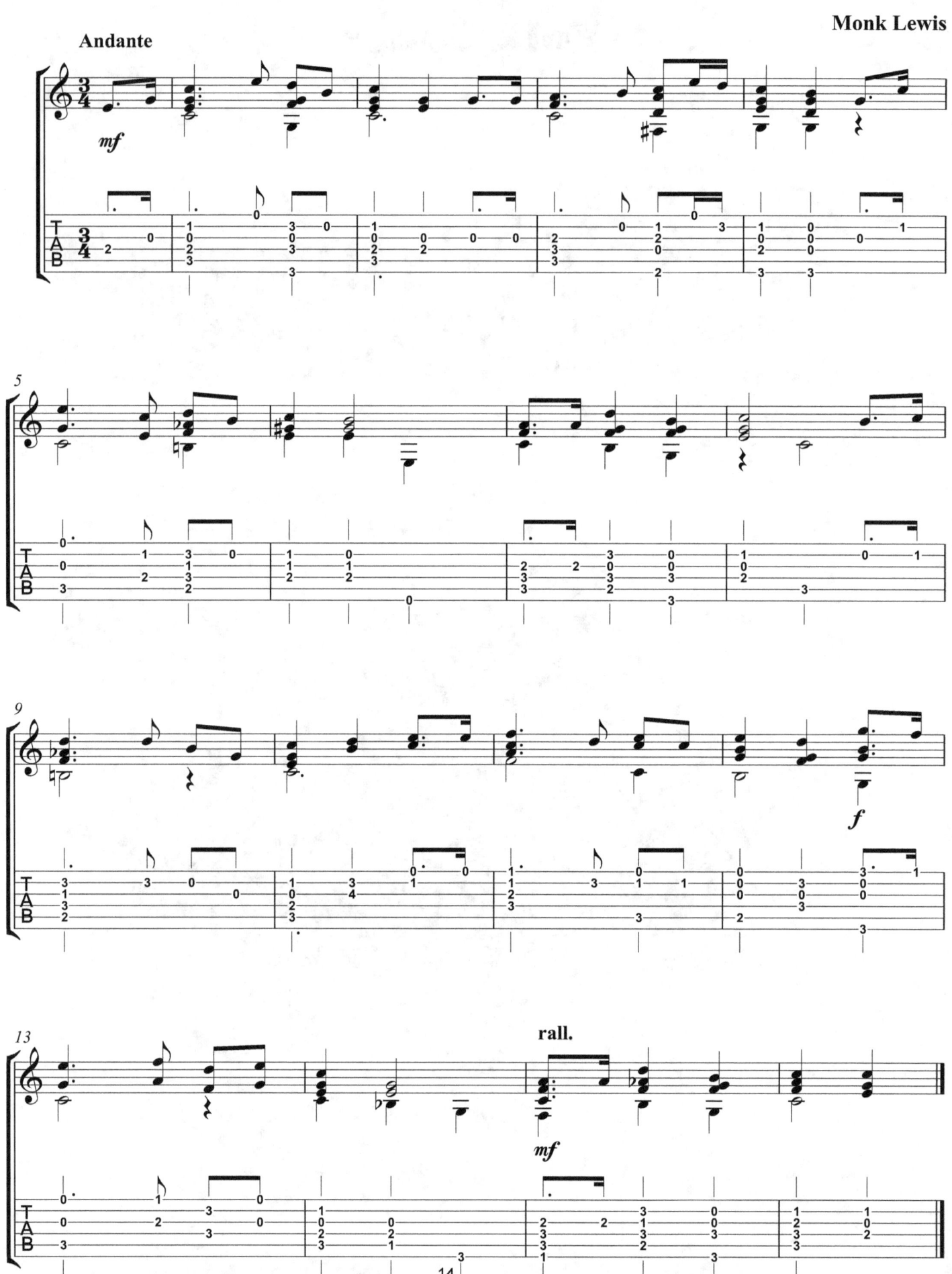

14

The Lark In The Clear Air

Samuel Ferguson

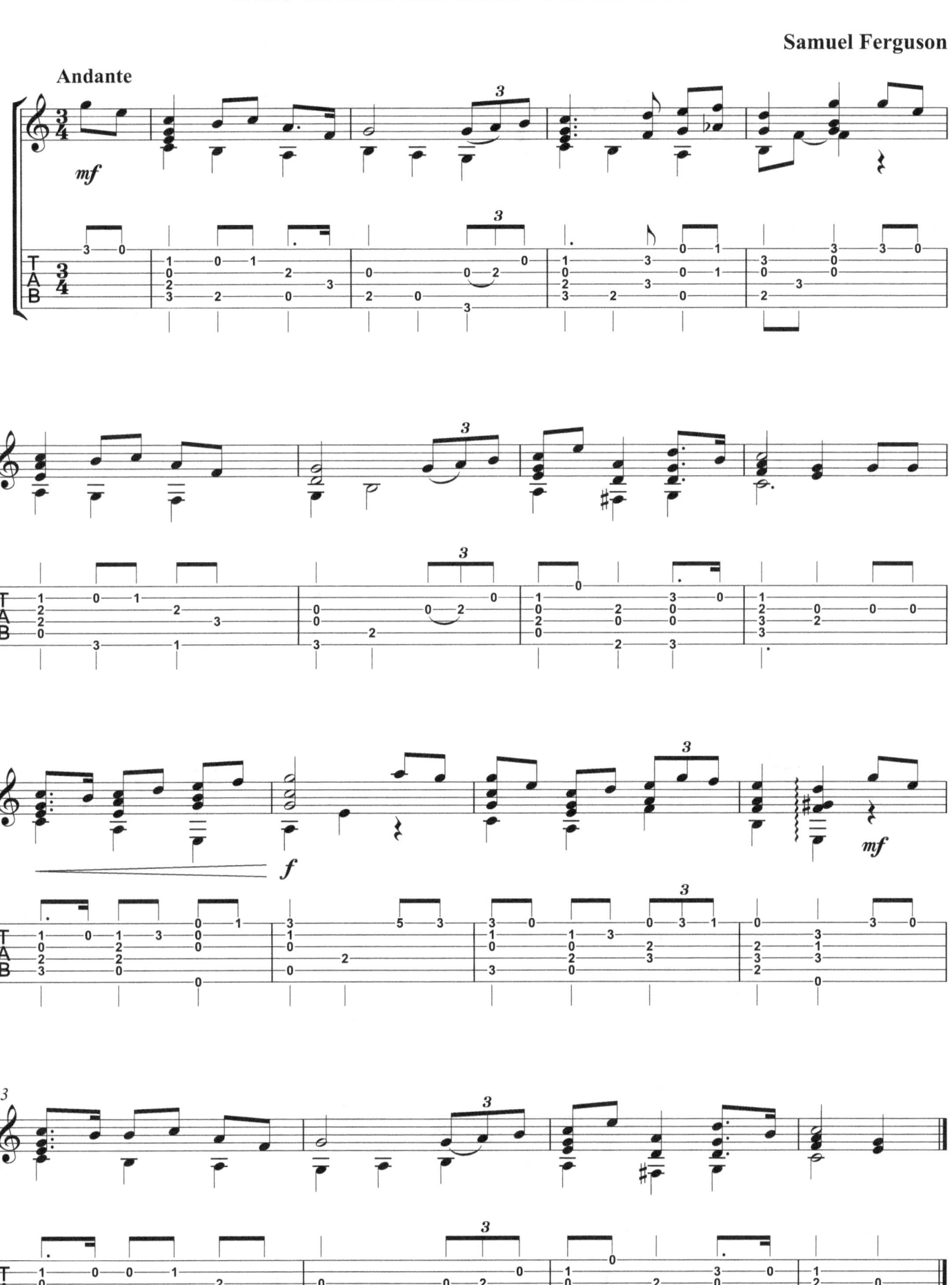

David Of The White Rock

Adagio

Welsh Air

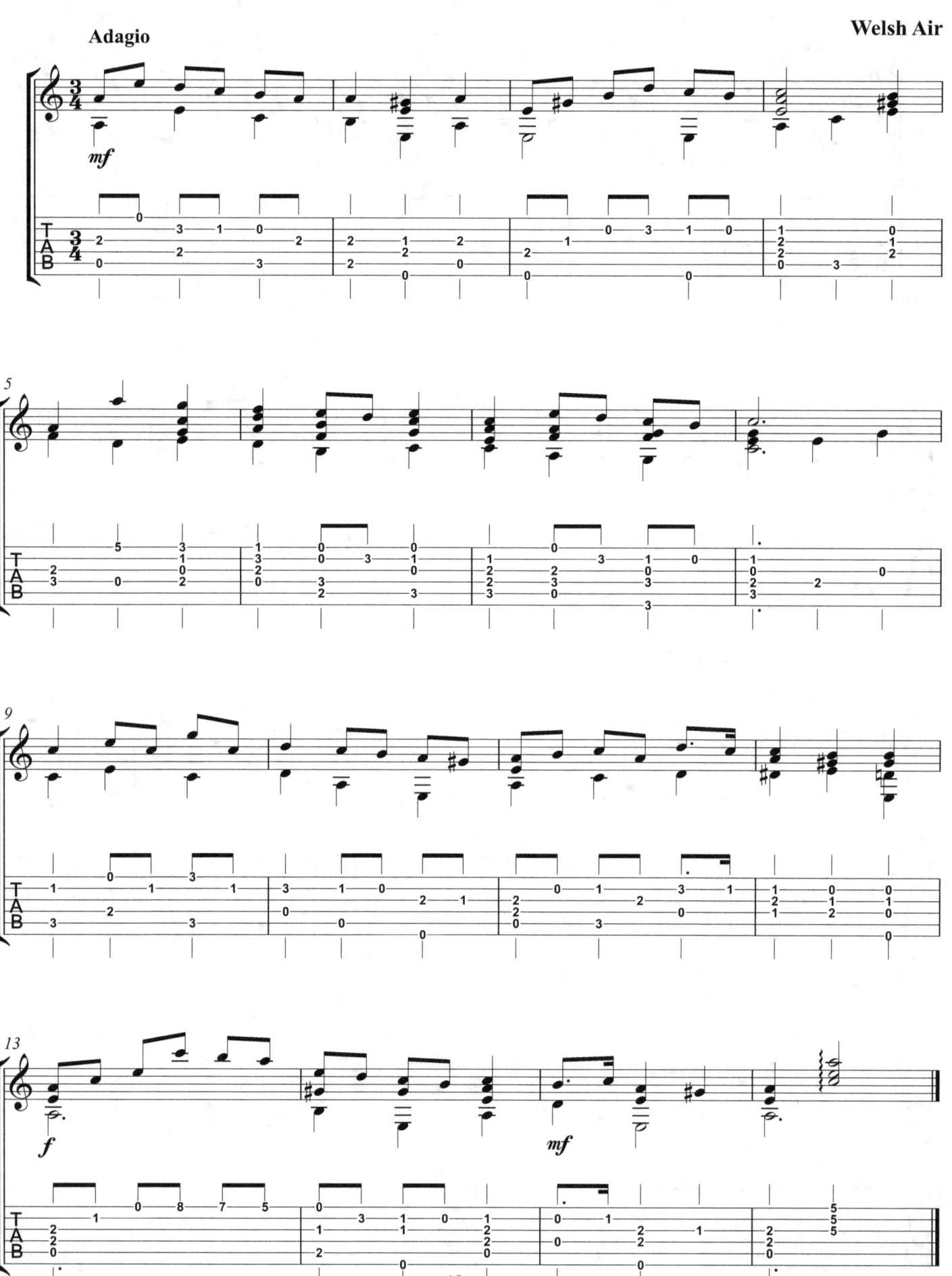

Believe Me, If All Those Endearing Young Charms

Thomas Moore

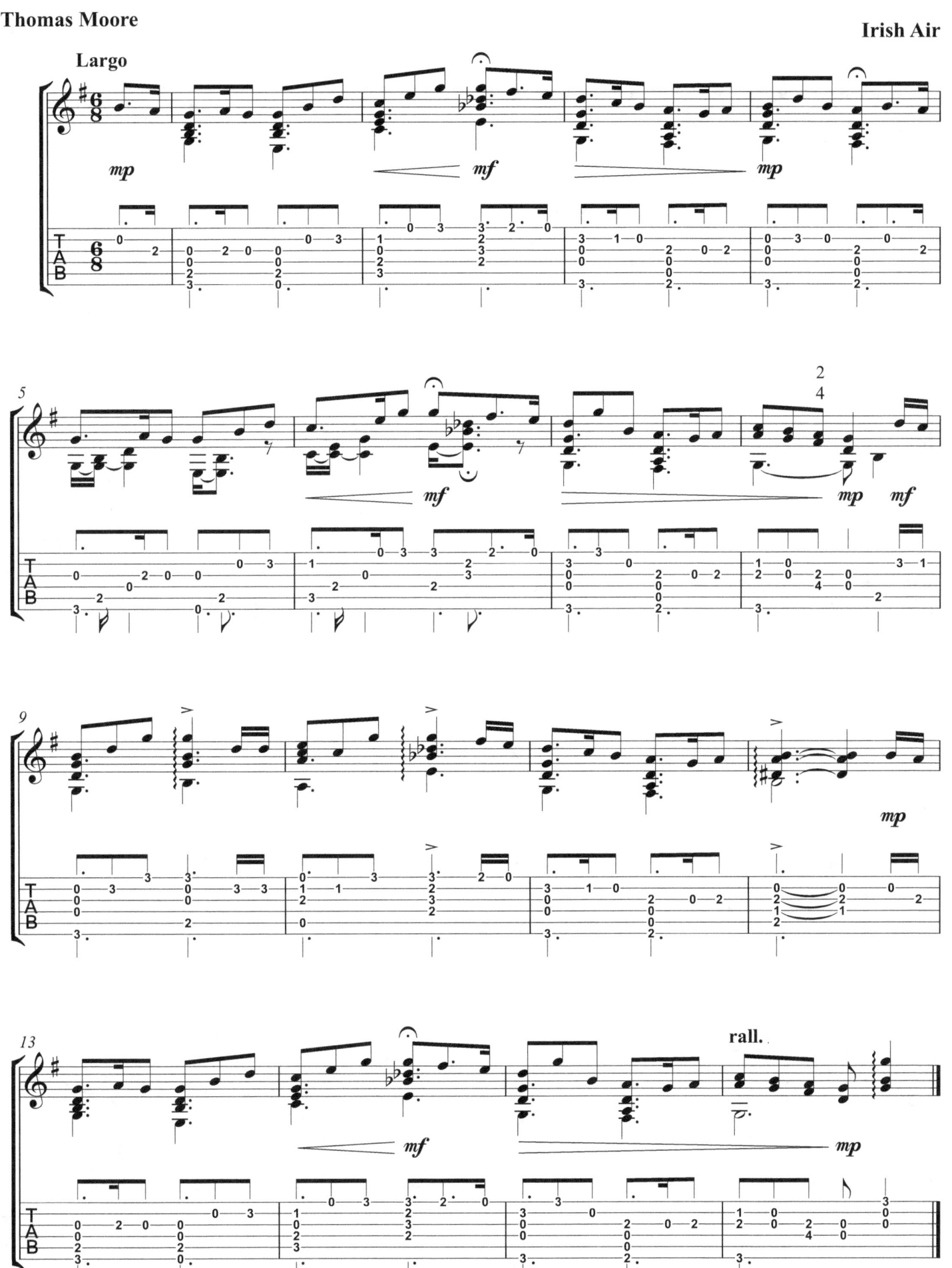

The Skye Boat Song

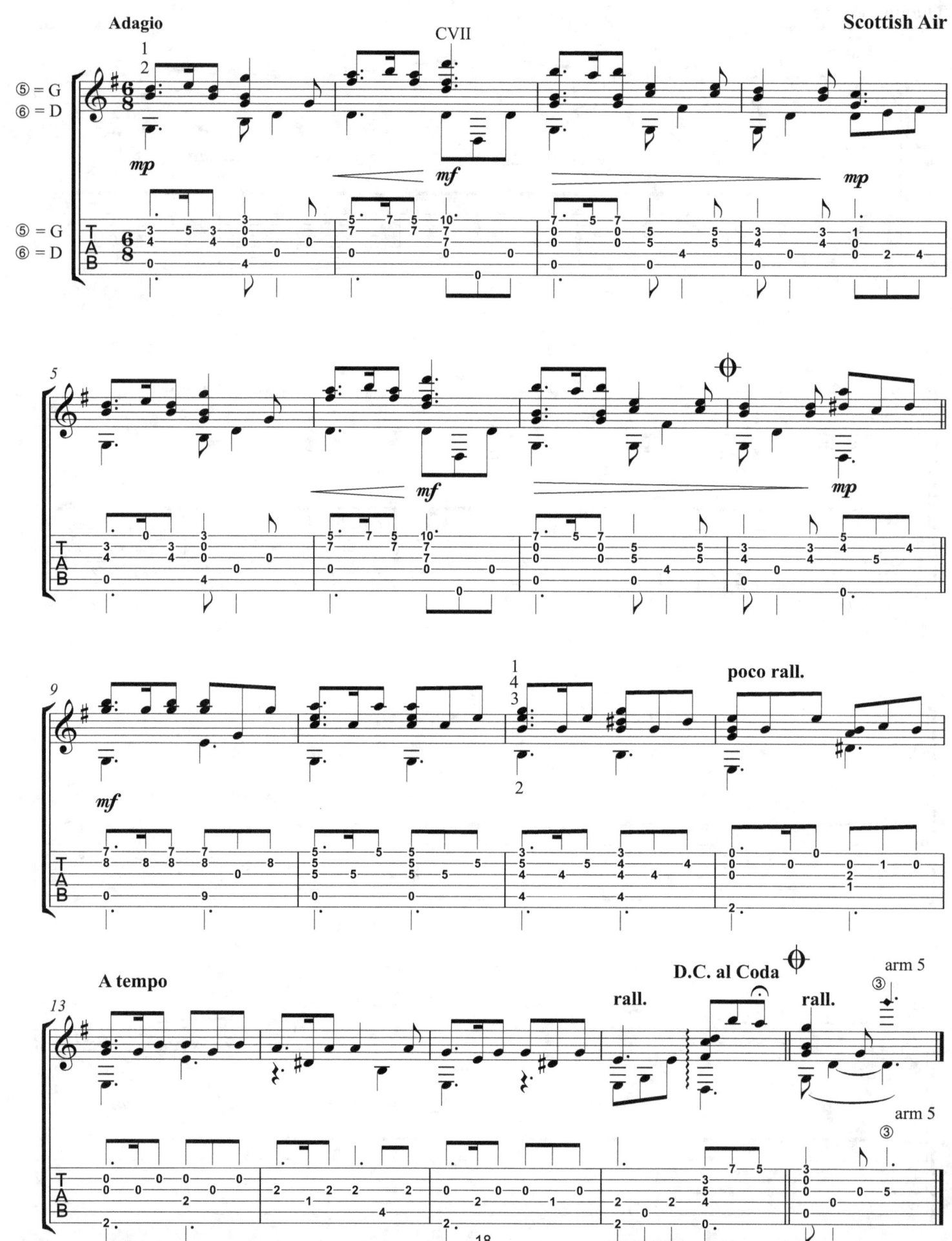

Annie Laurie

Lady Jane Scott

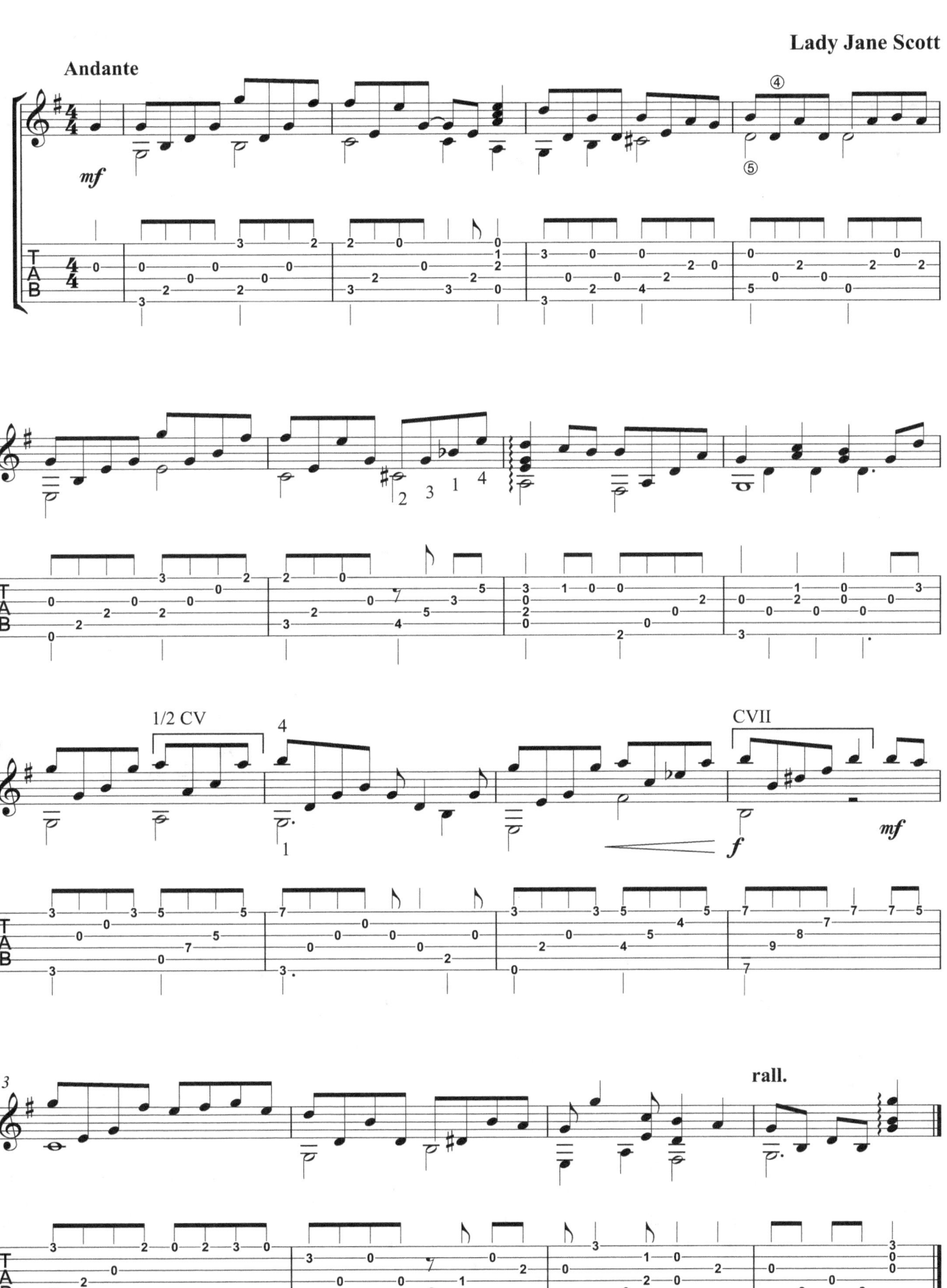

Deep River

American Spiritual

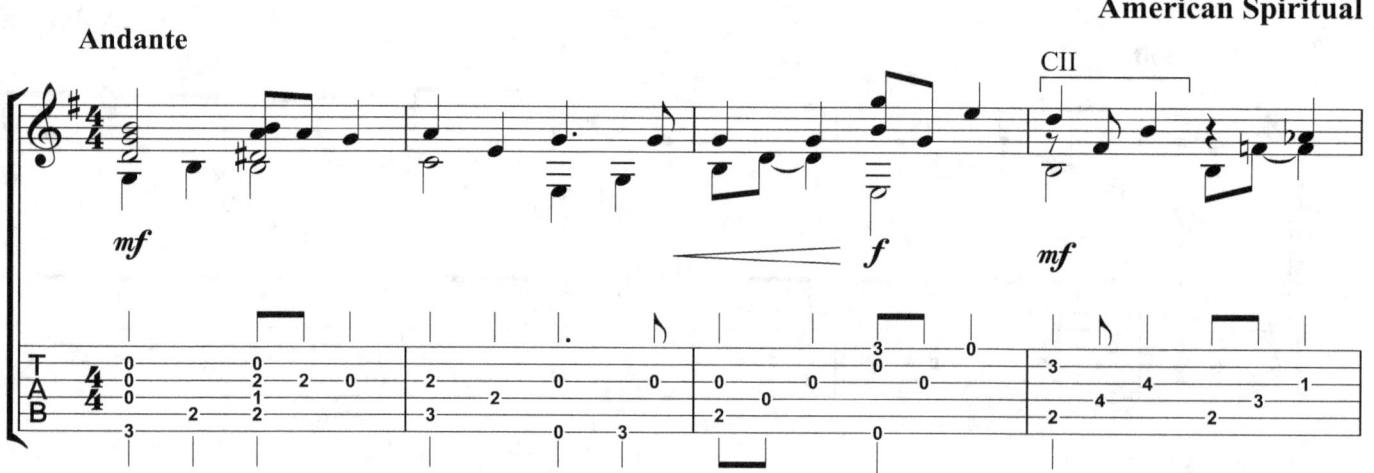

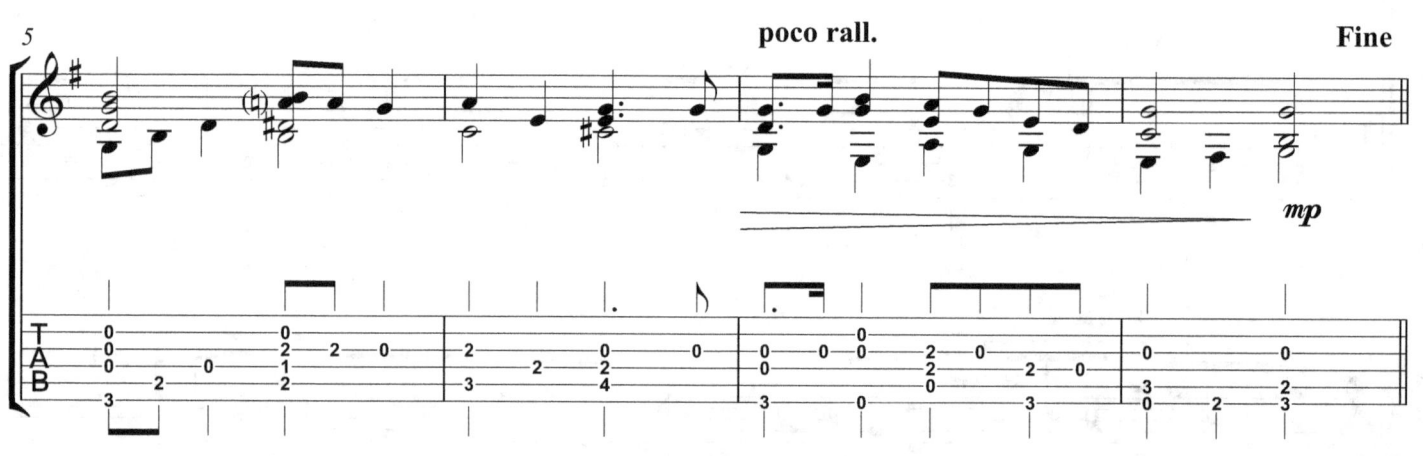

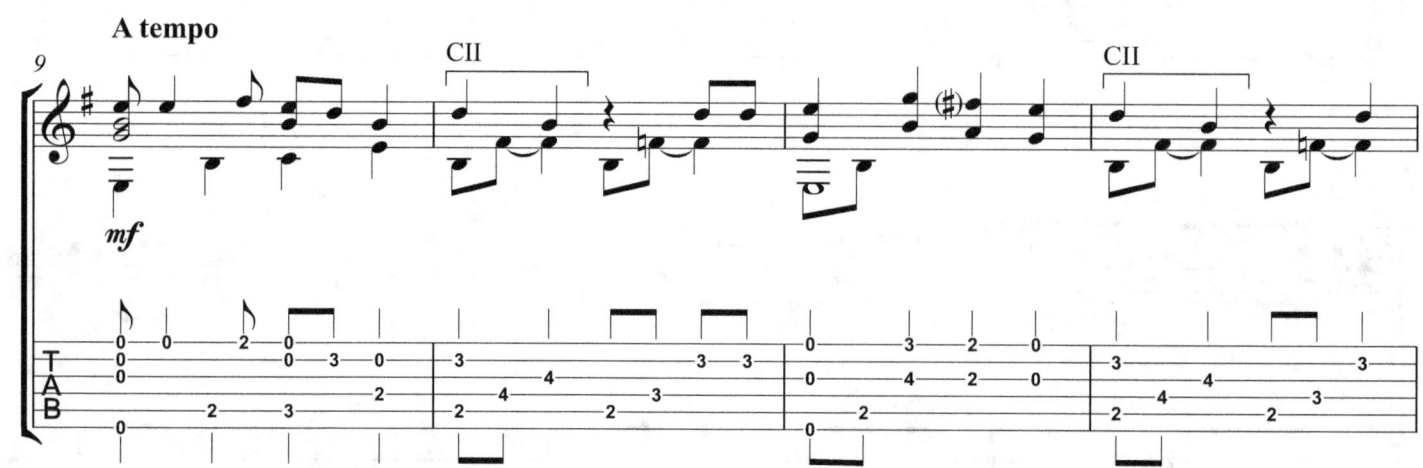

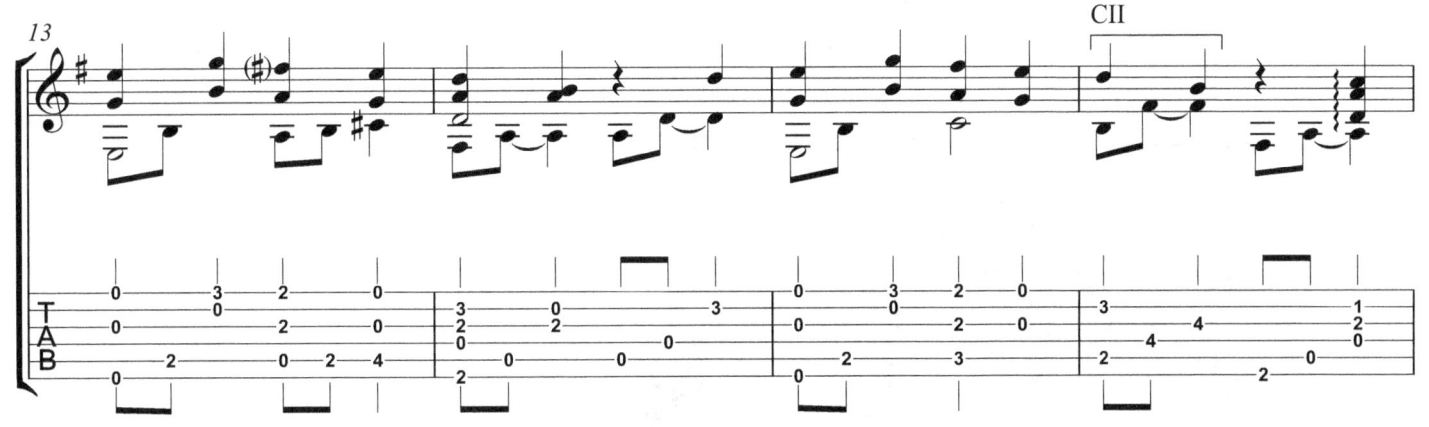

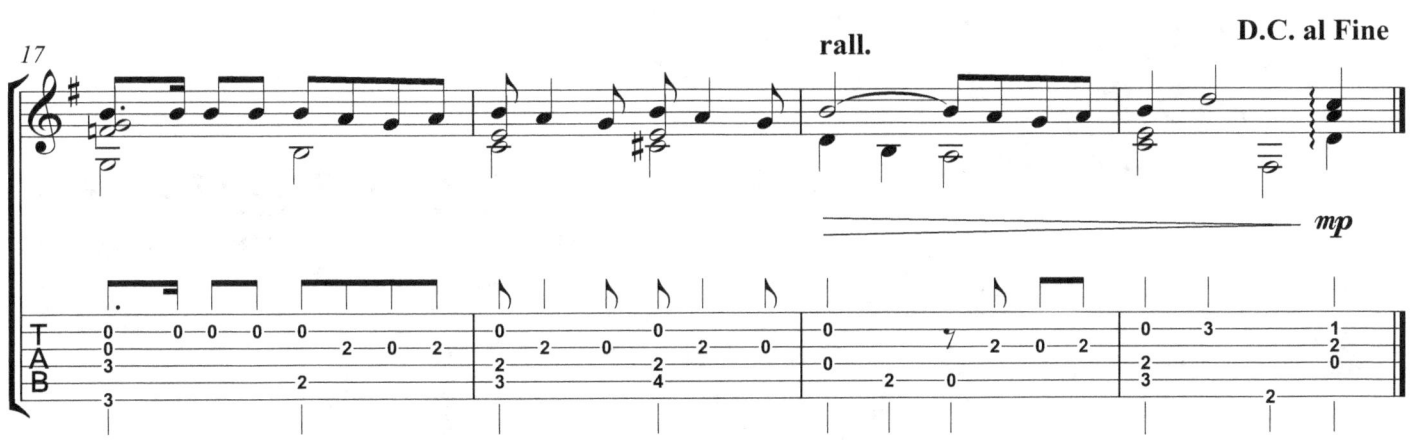

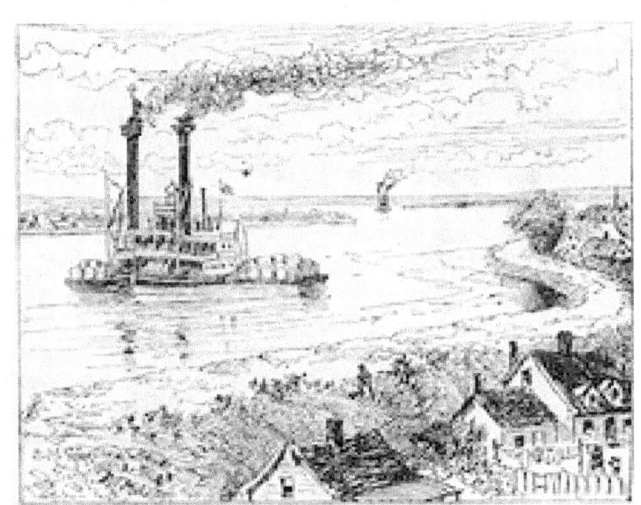

Images of the Great Irish Tenor, John McCormack (1883-1945), performer of many songs in this book: Believe Me, If All Those Endearing Young Charms; Annie Laurie; Jeanie With The Light Brown Hair; At Dawning; The Lark In The Clear Air.

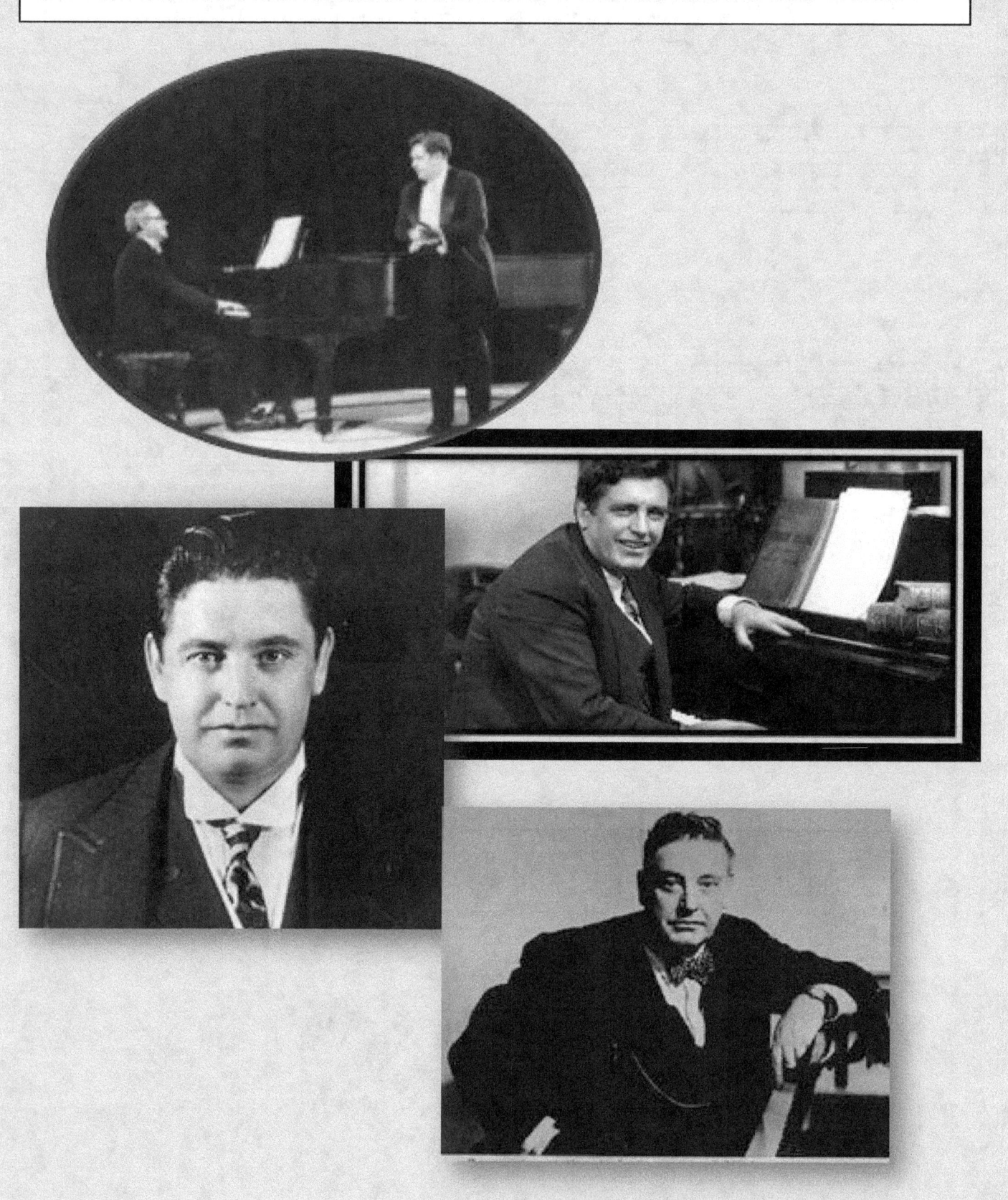

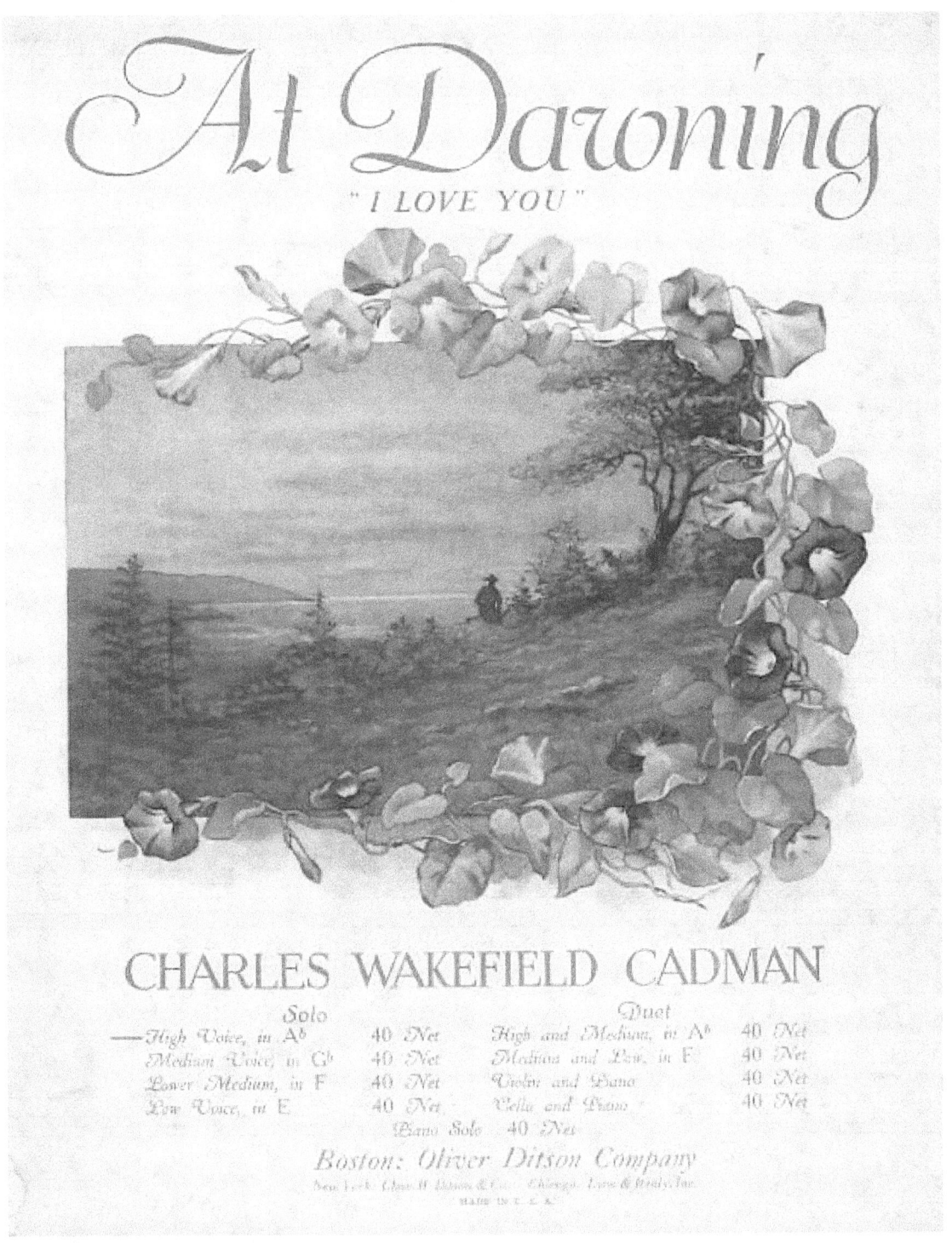

At Dawning

Charles Wakefield Cadman

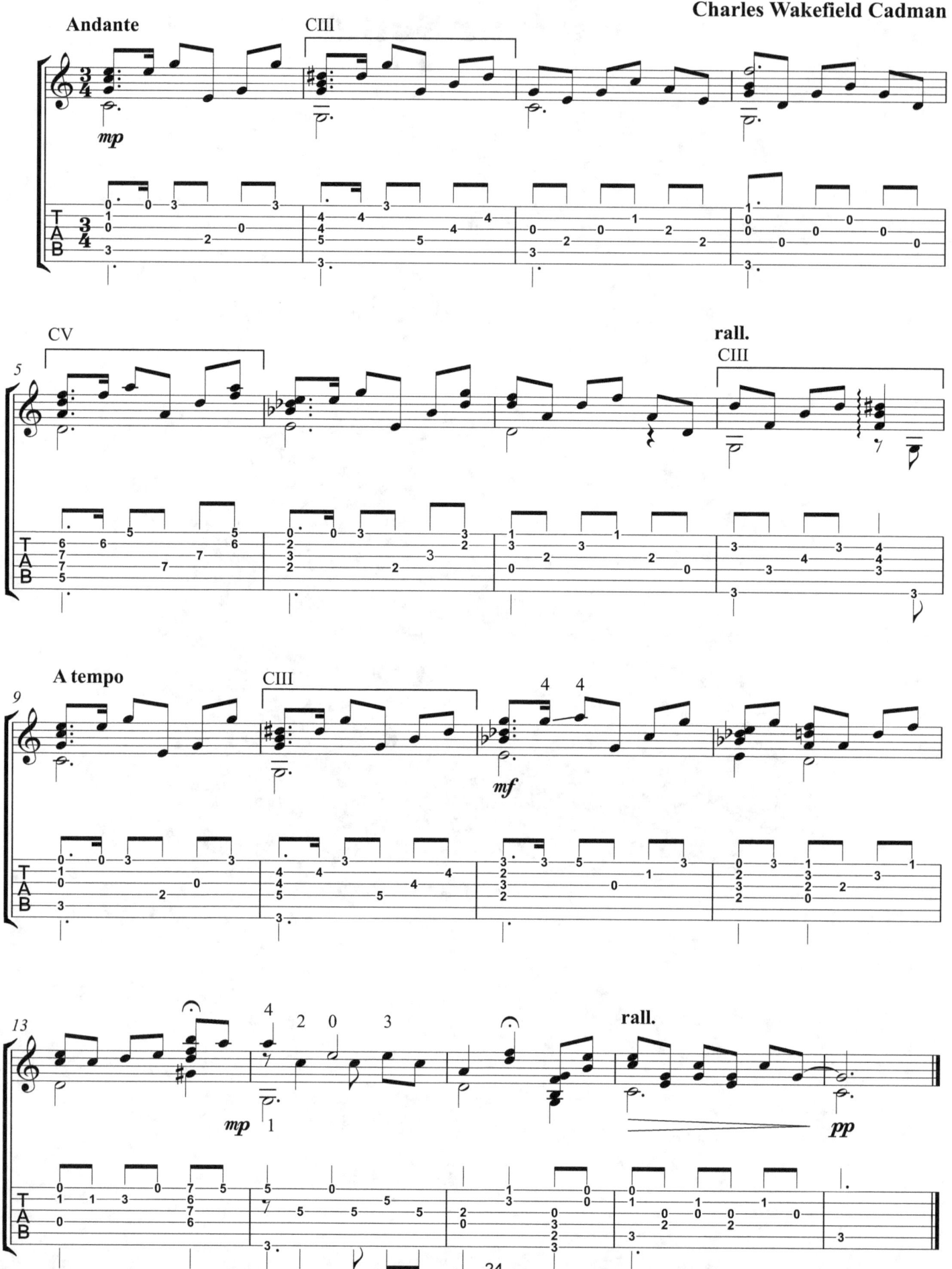

I Love You Truly

Carrie Jacobs Bond

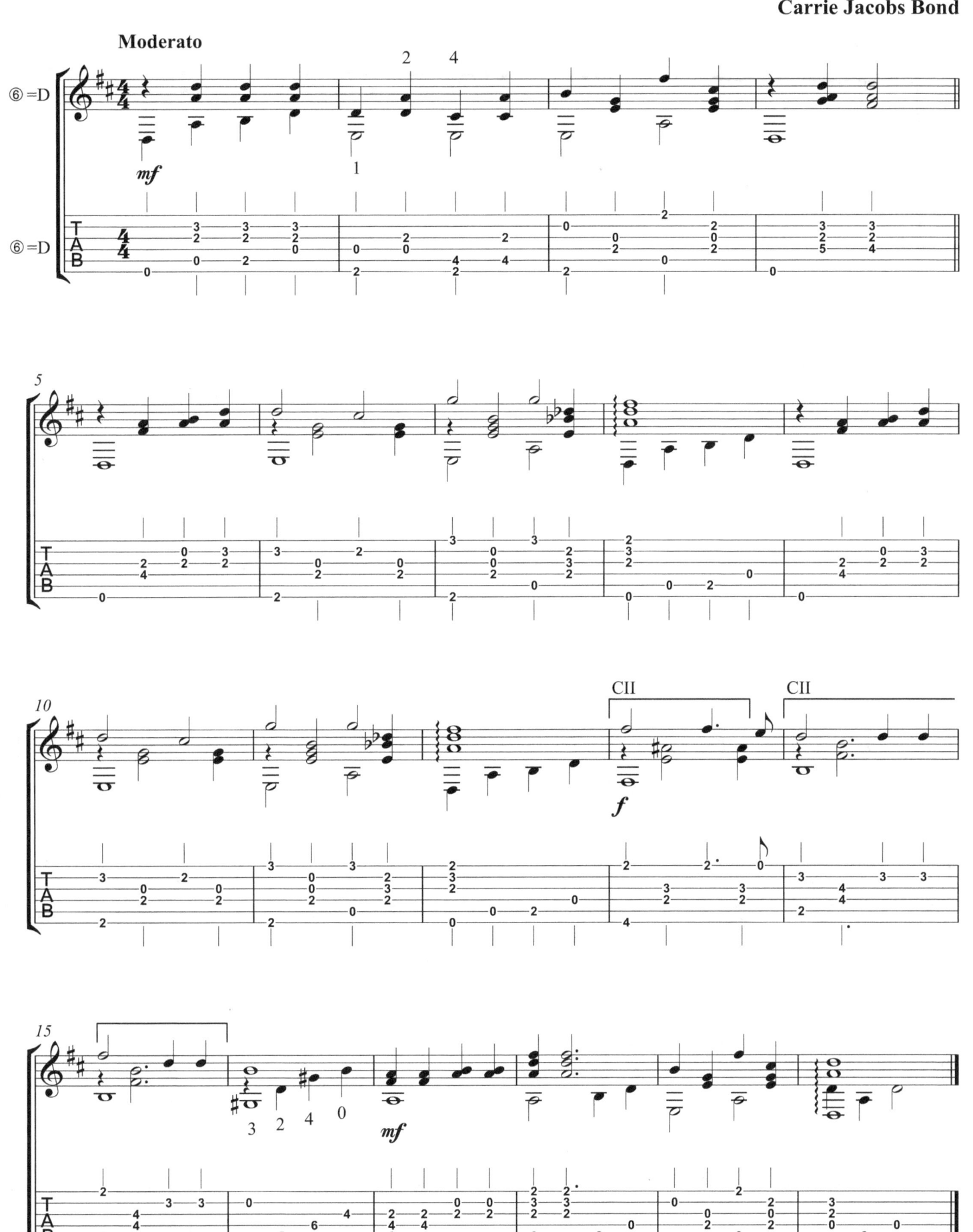

Kiss Me Again

Henry Blossom

Victor Herbert

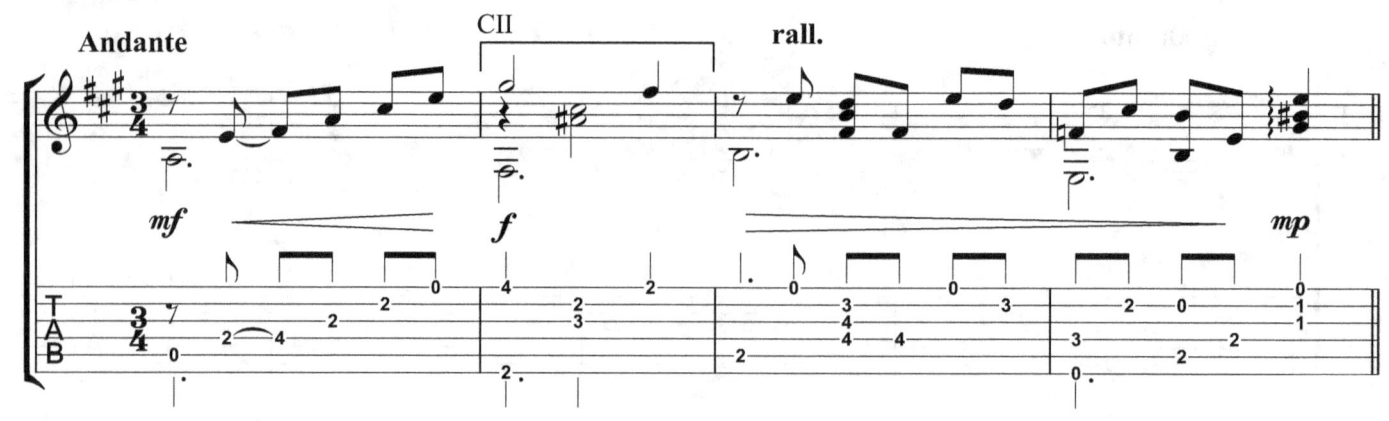

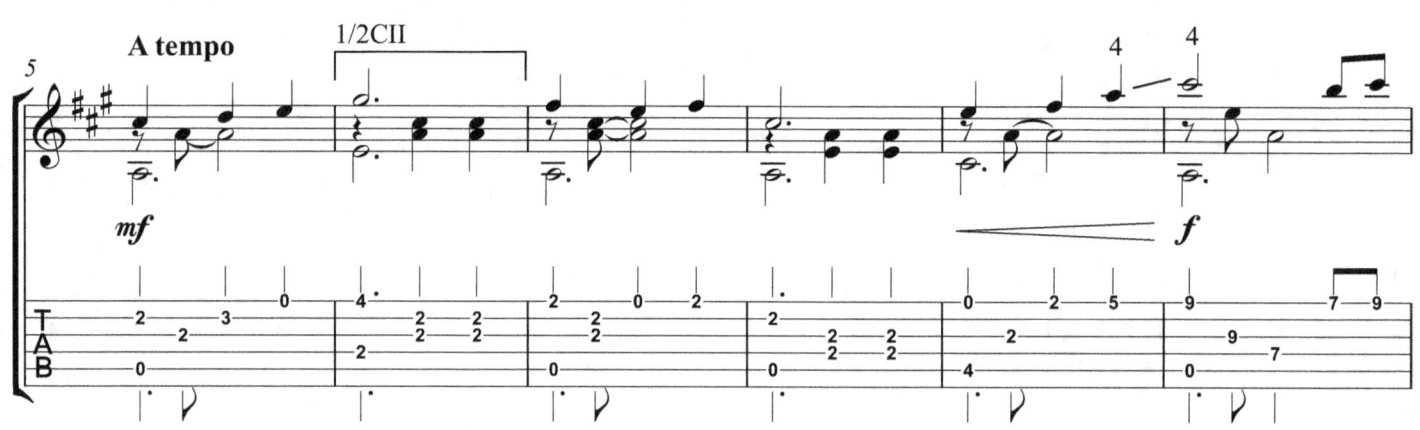

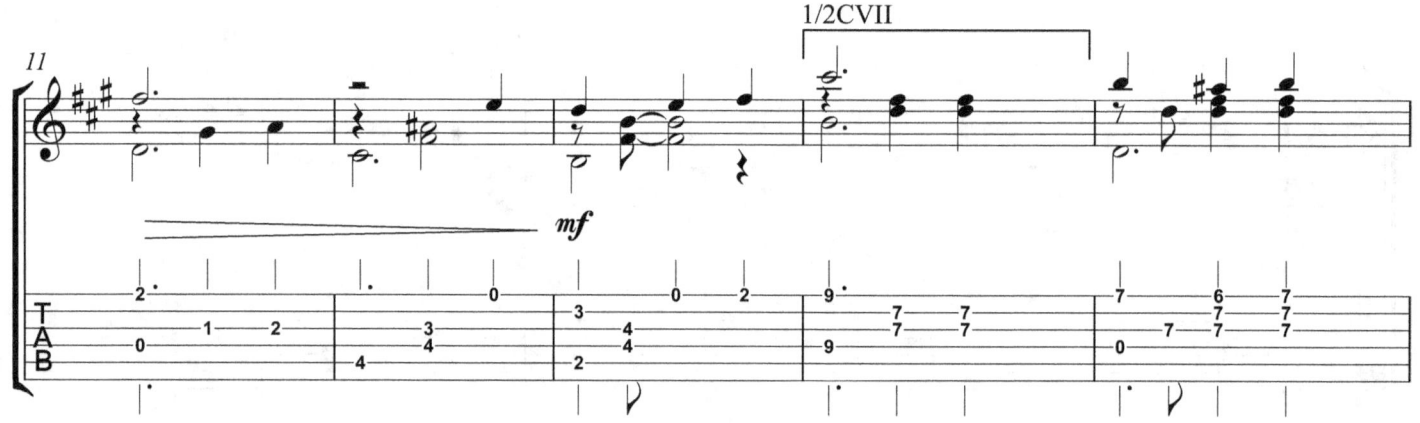

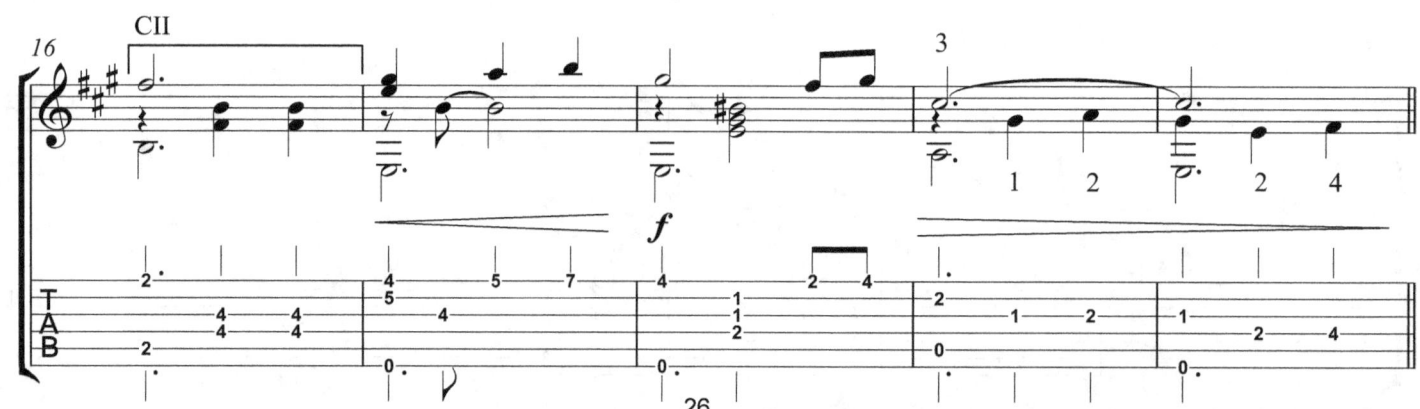

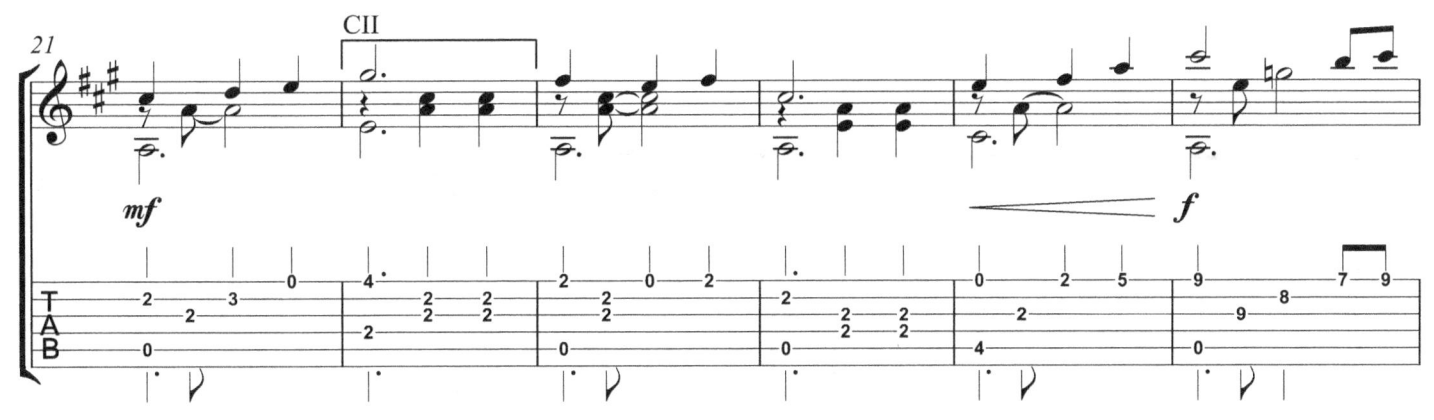

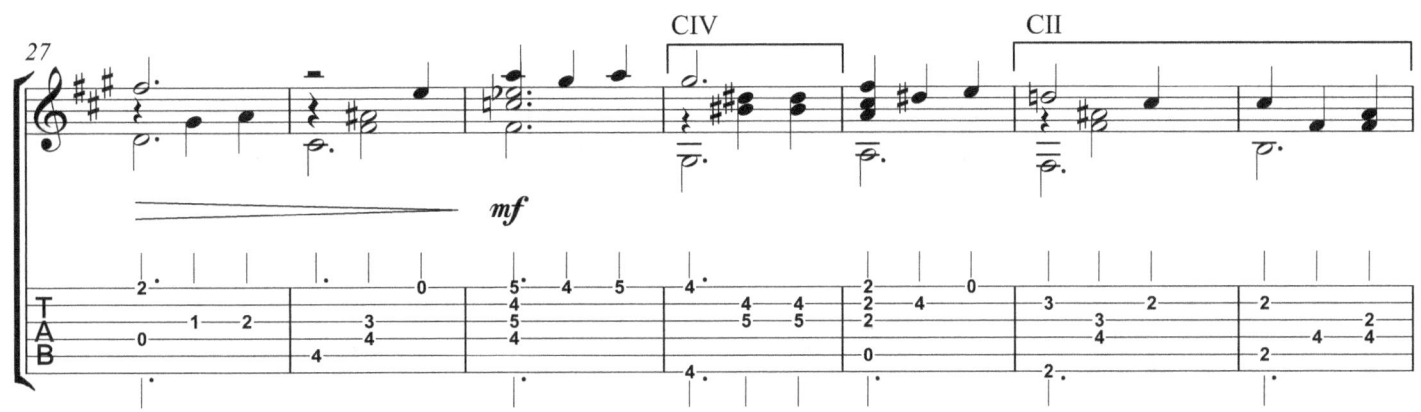

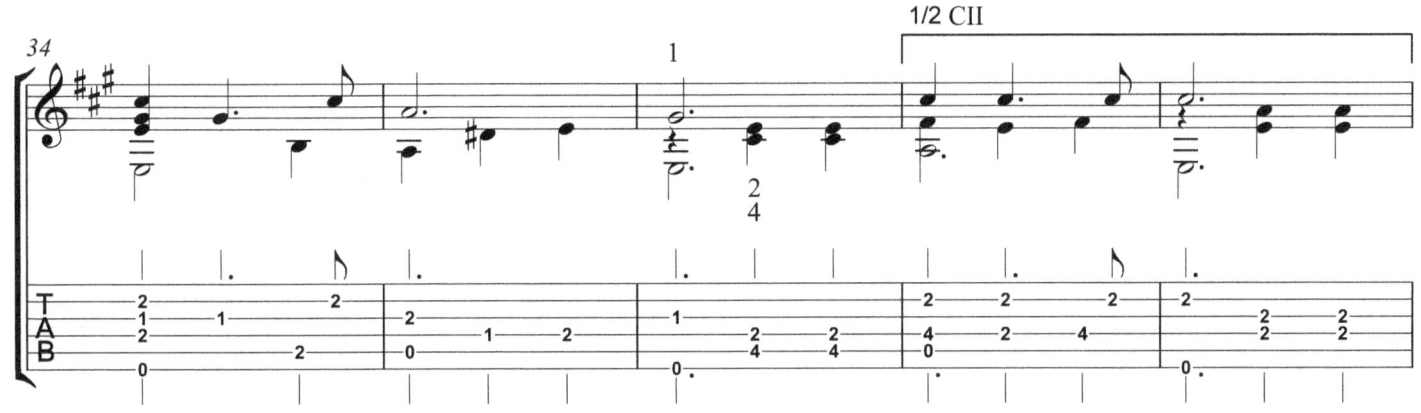

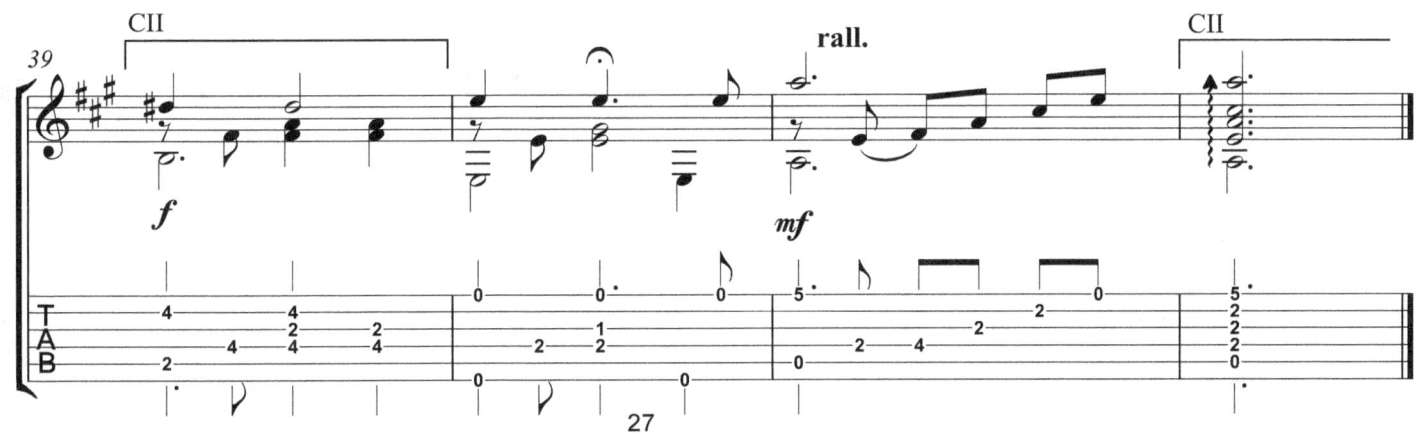

My Wild Irish Rose

Chauncey Olcott

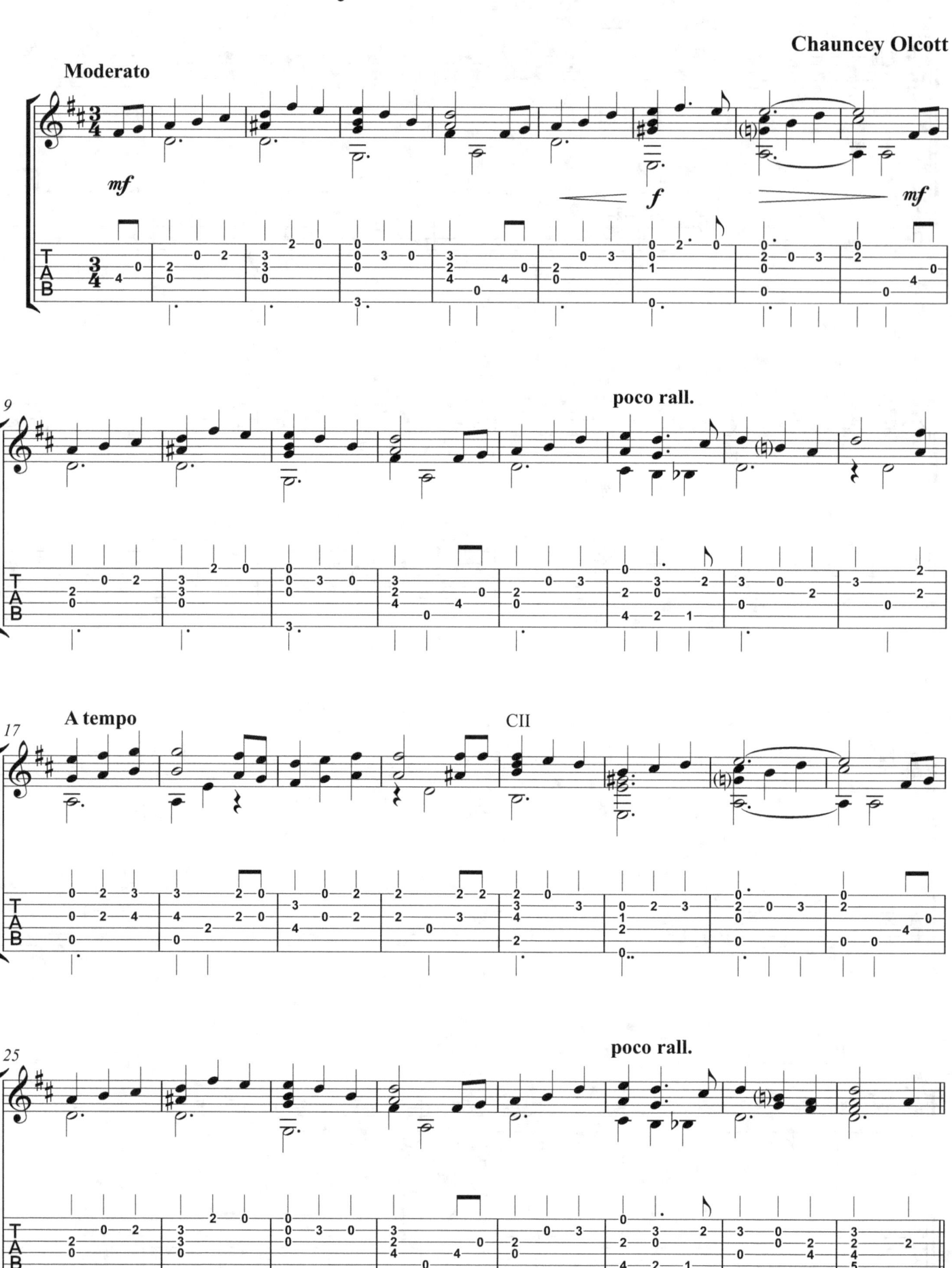

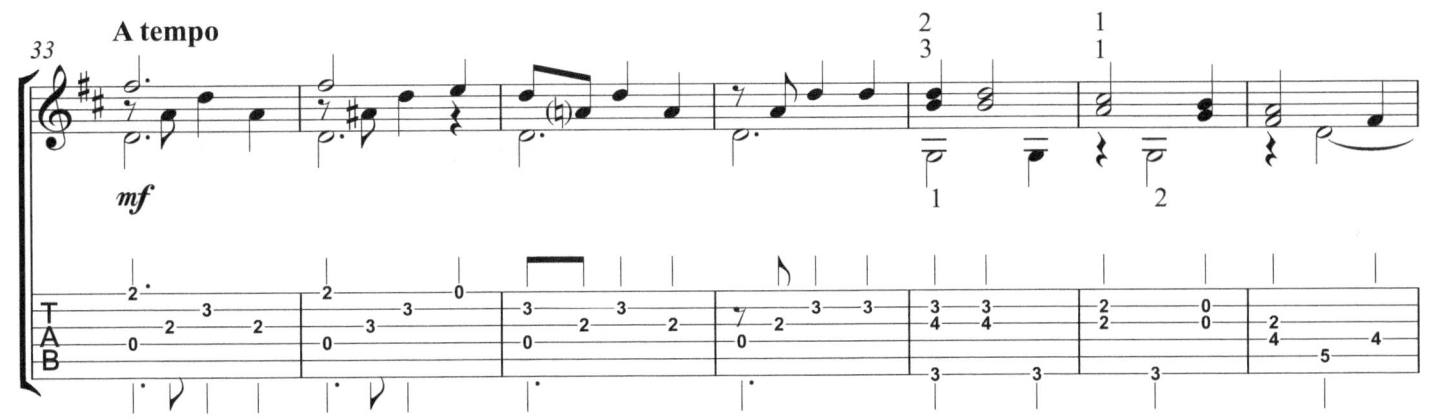

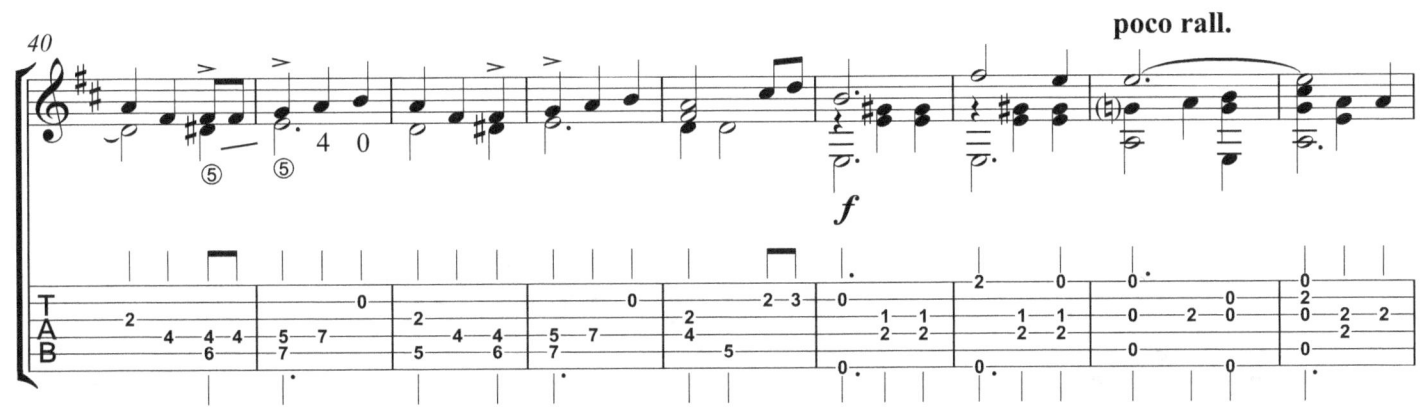

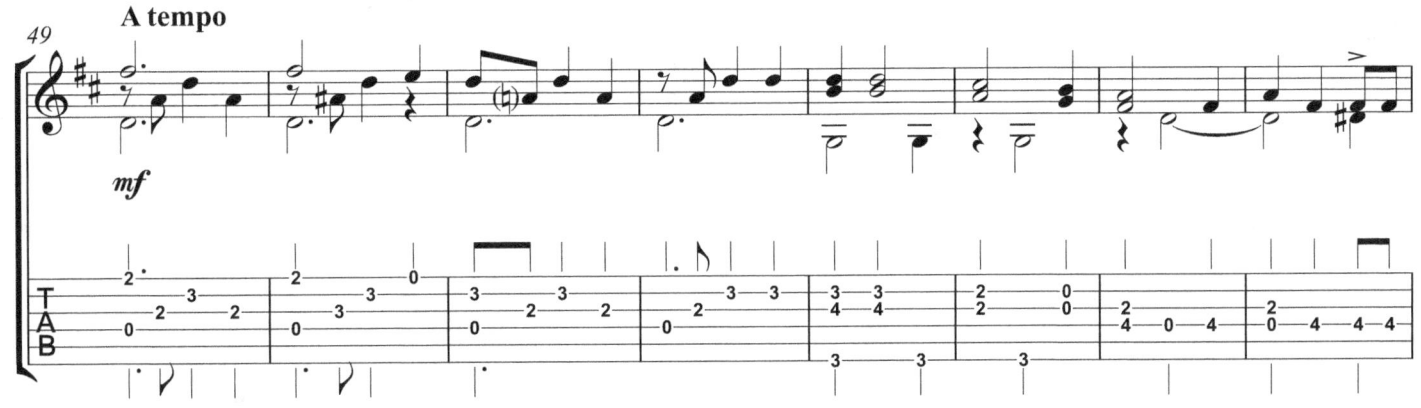

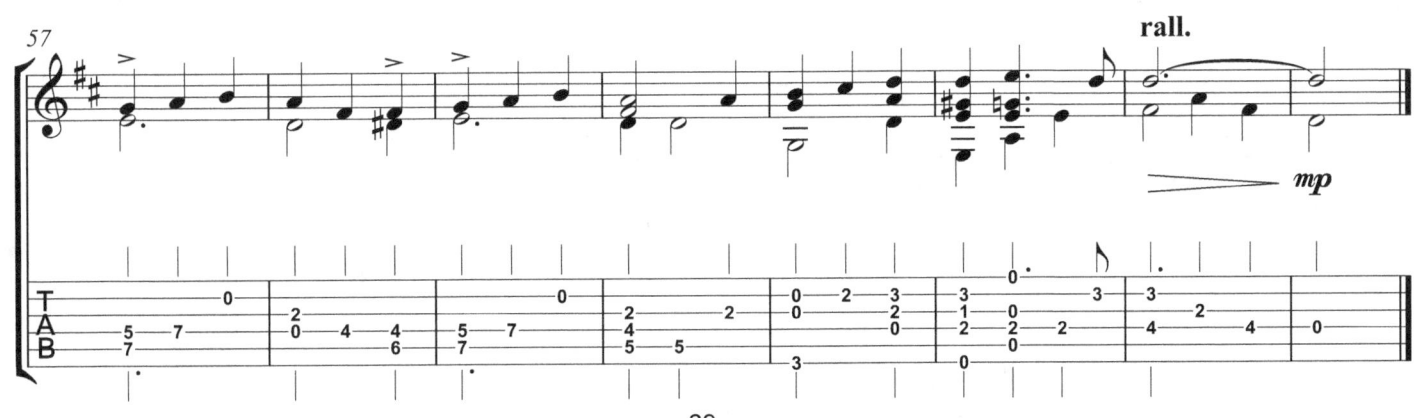

Love's Old Sweet Song

G. Clifton Bingham

James L. Molloy

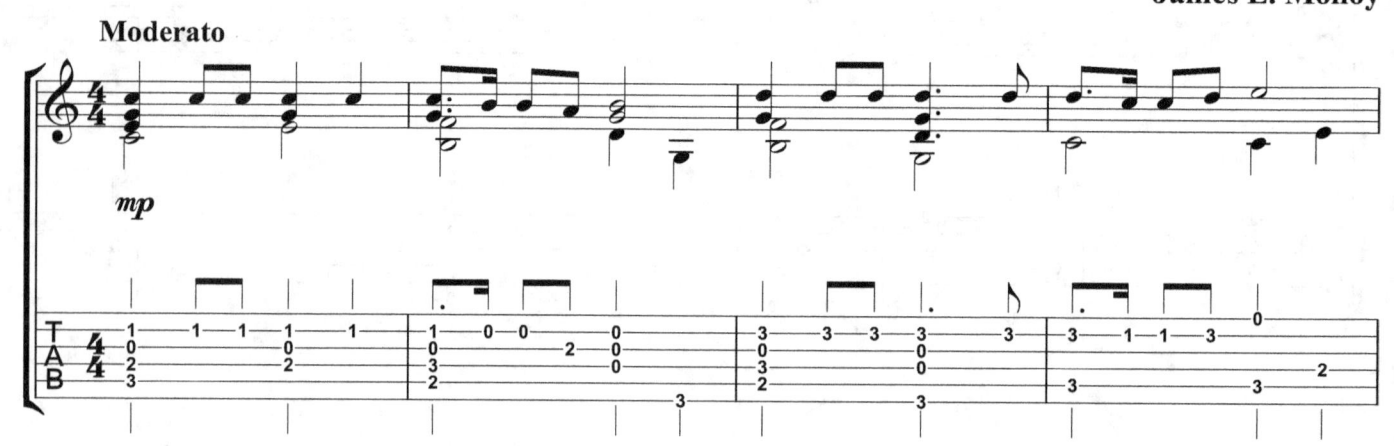

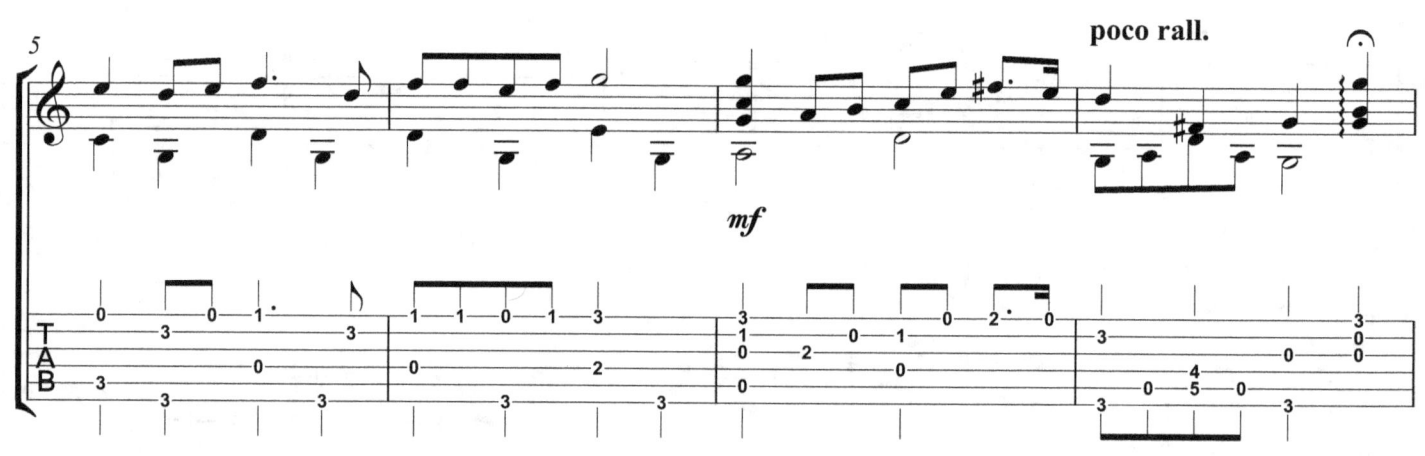

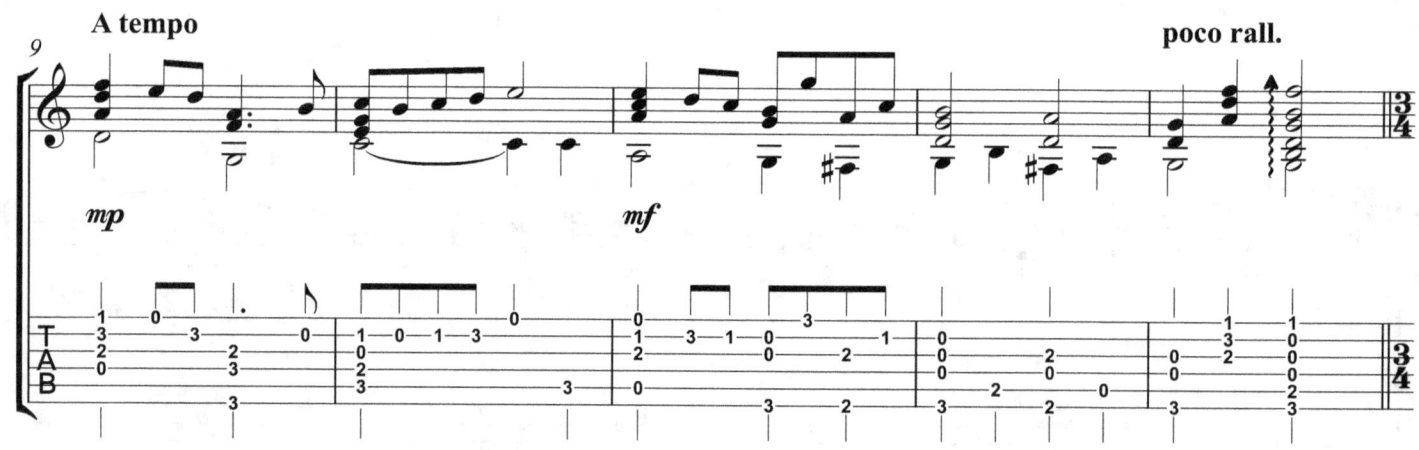

A tempo

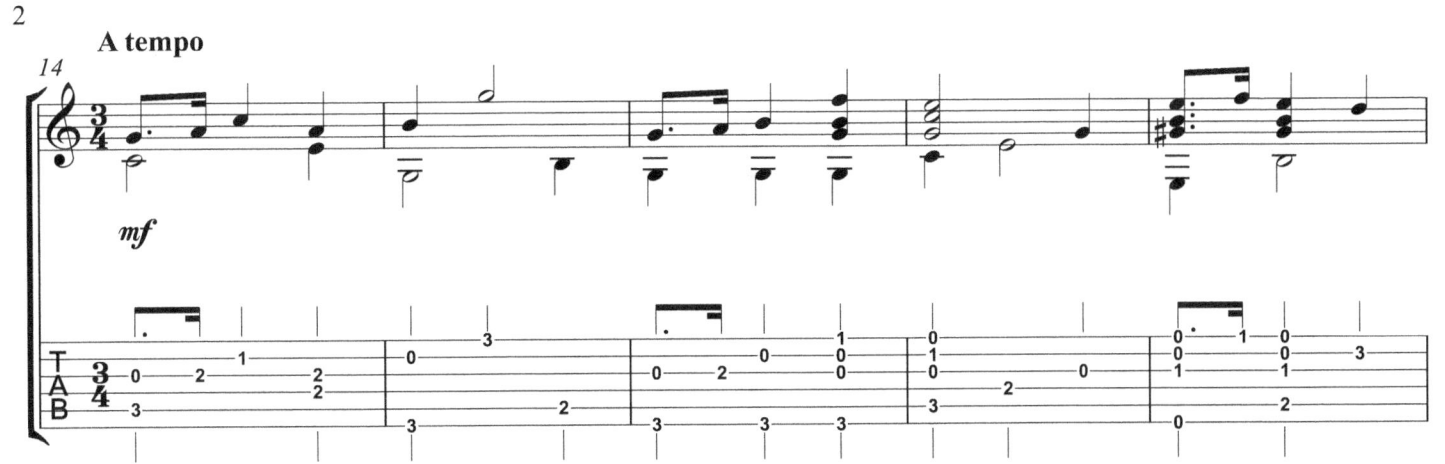

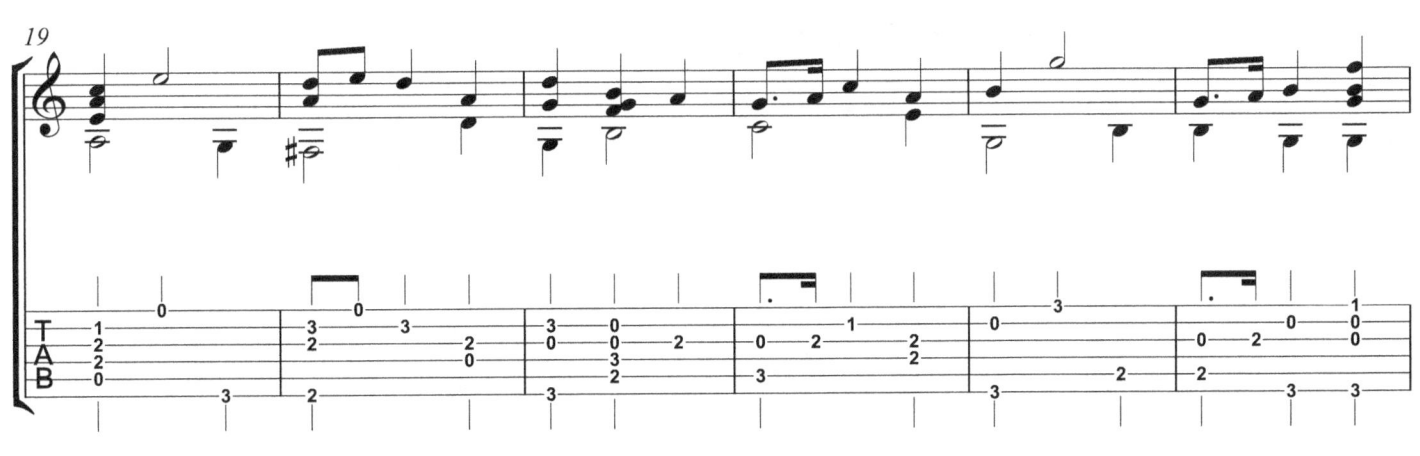

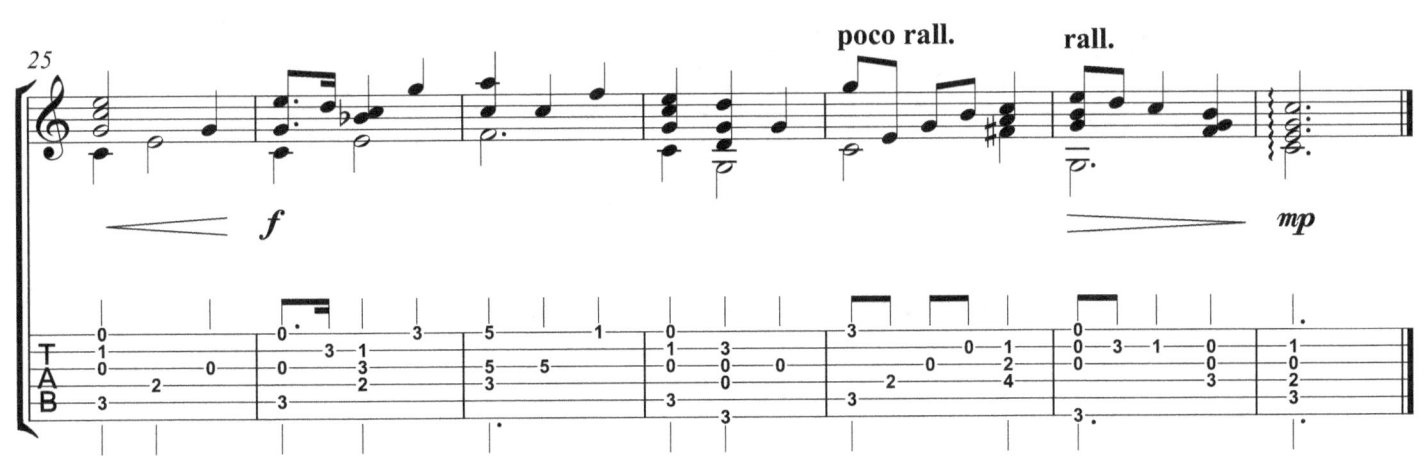

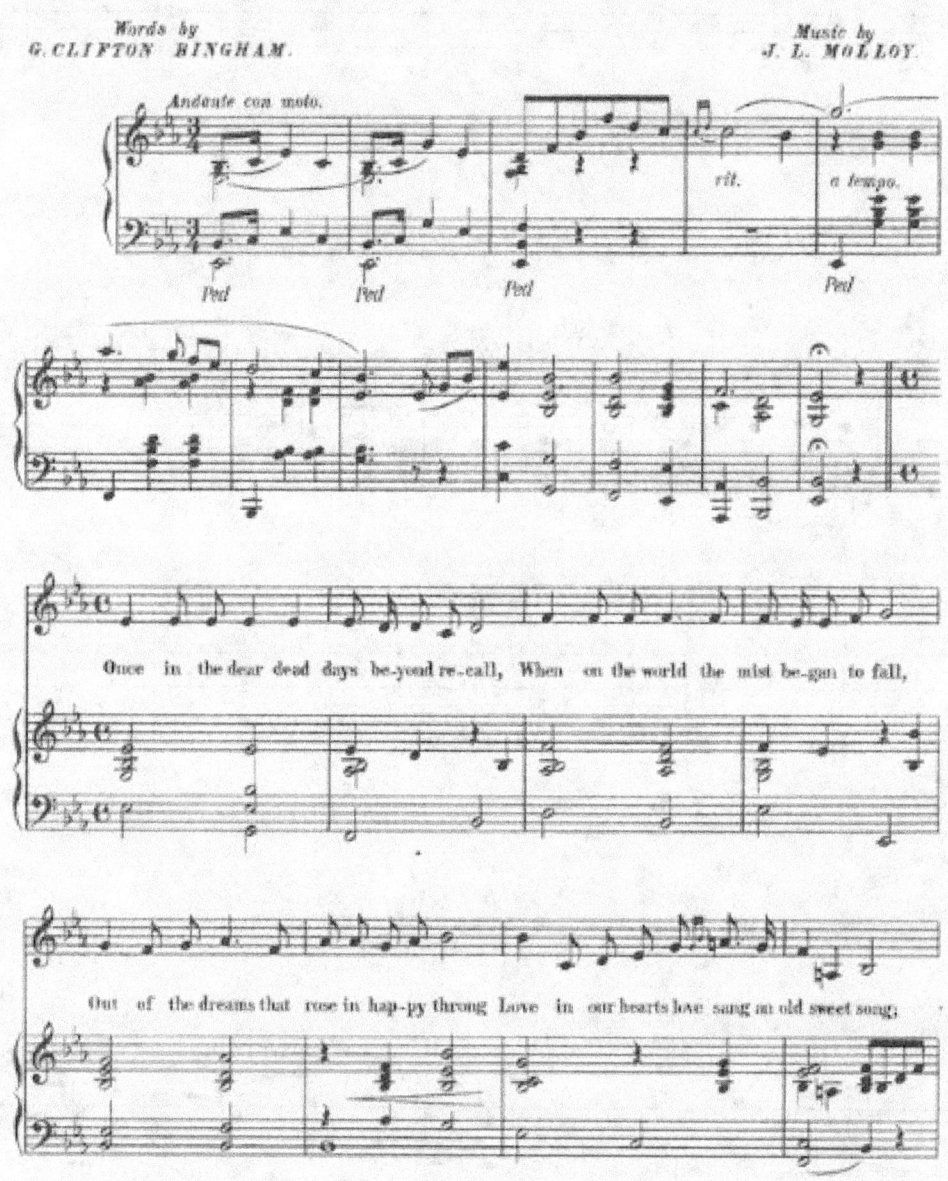

The original sheet music for Love's Old Sweet Song (1884)

Classical Arrangements

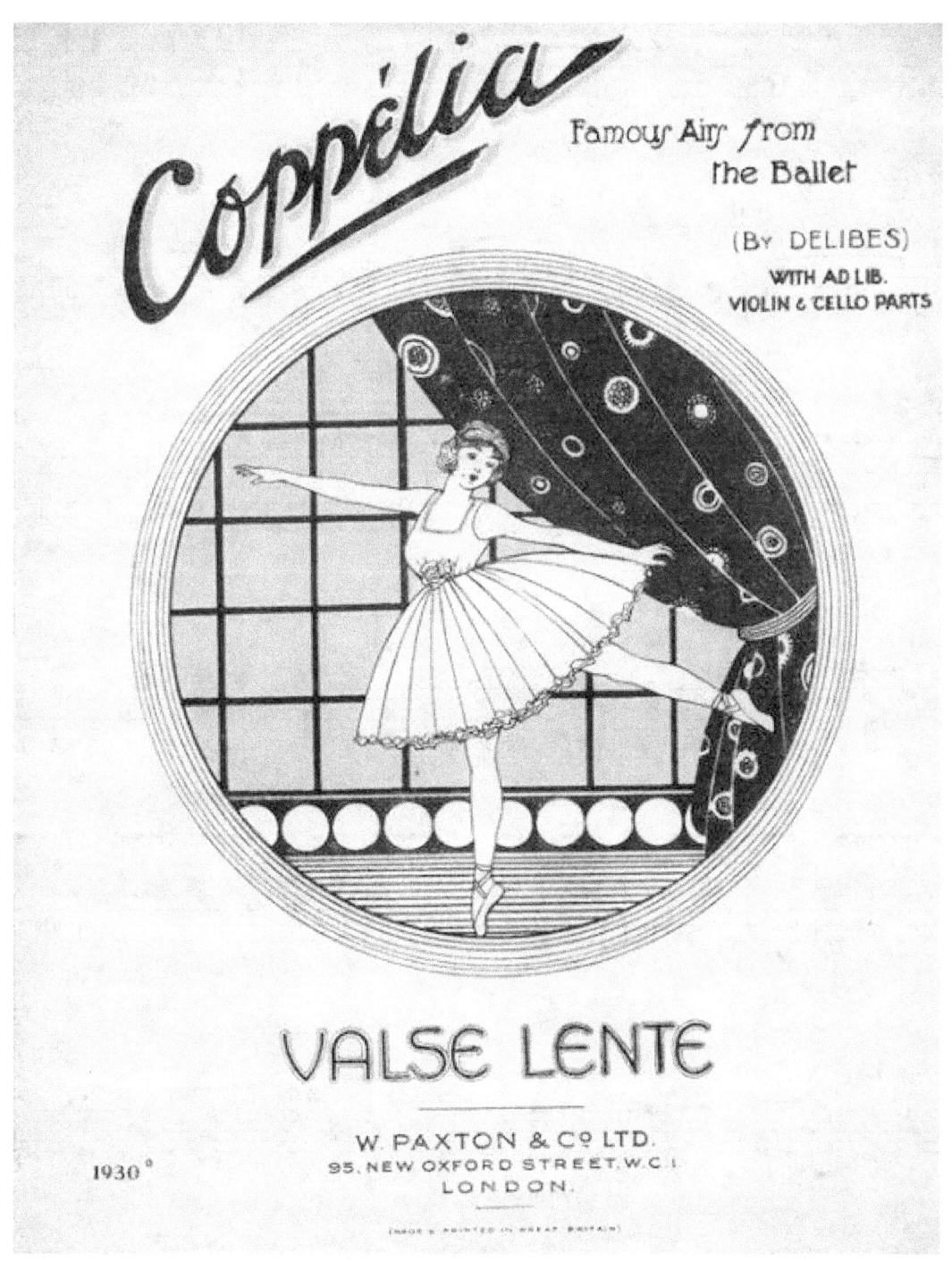

Chanson De Matin

Edward Elgar

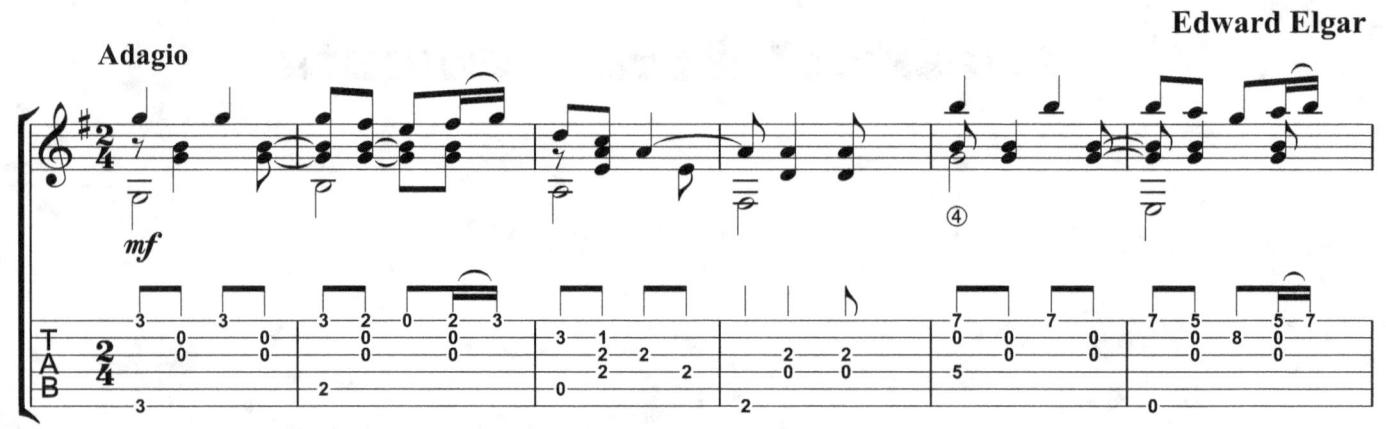

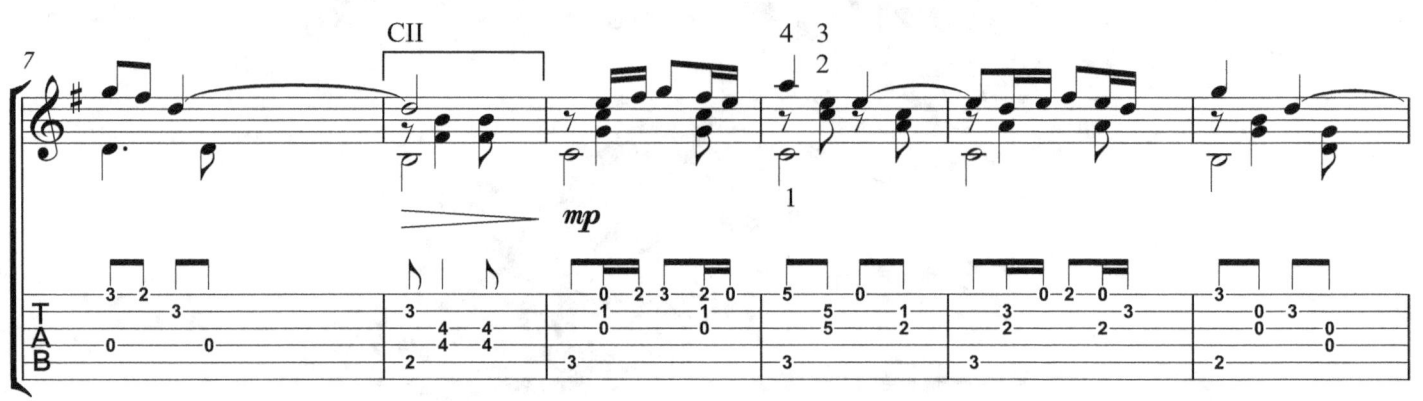

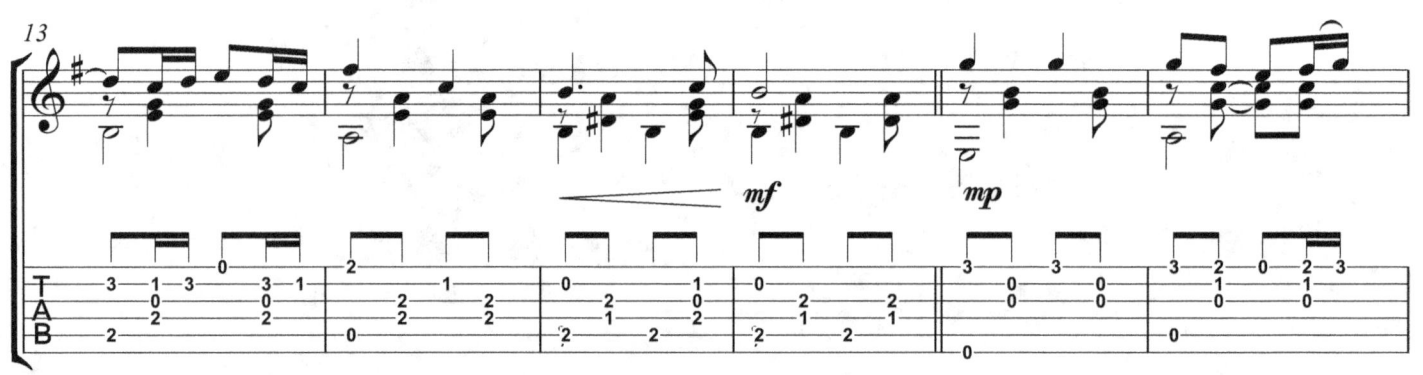

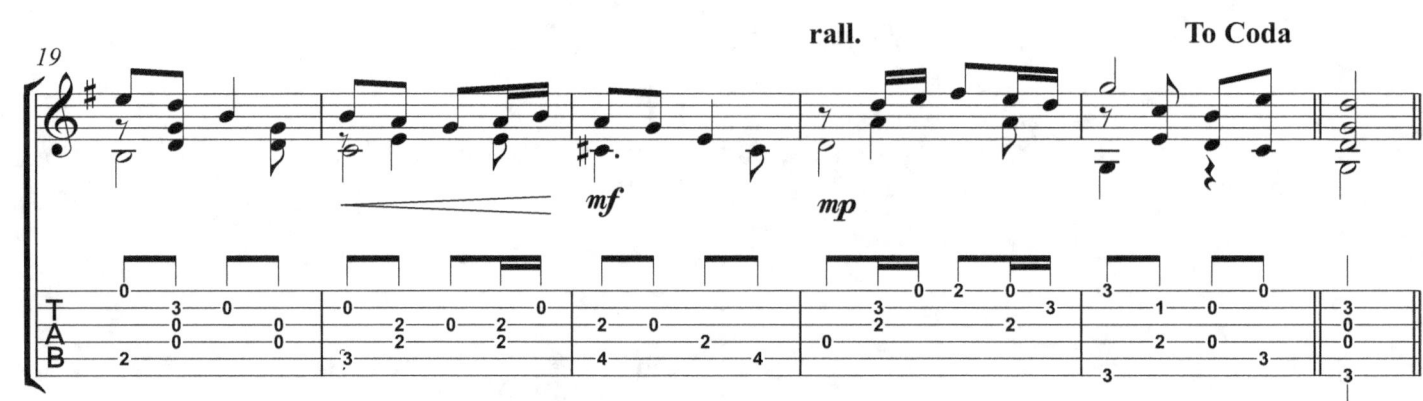

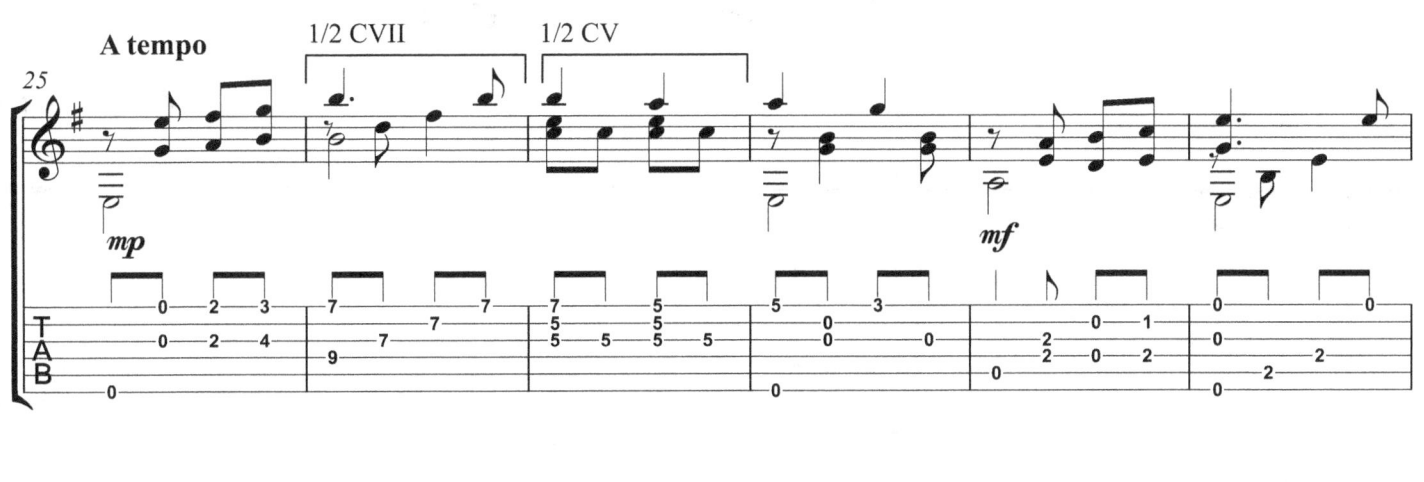

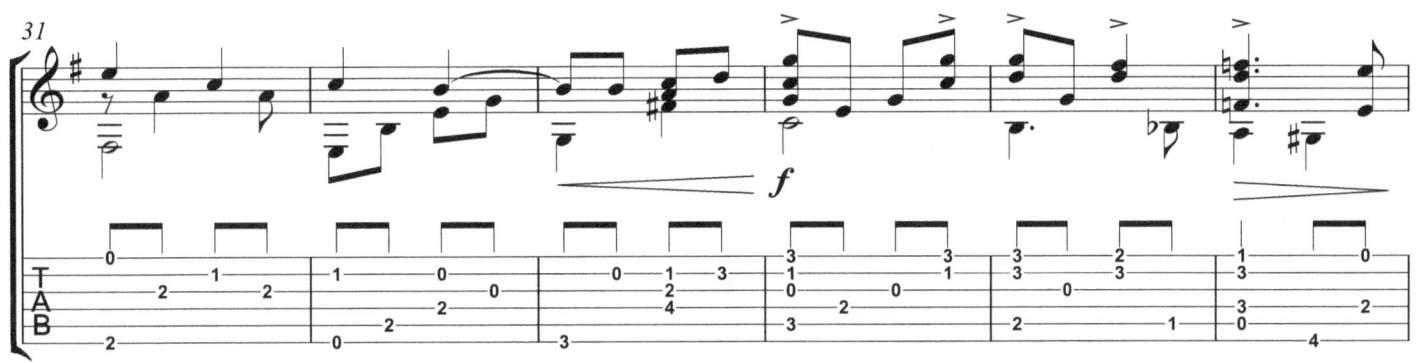

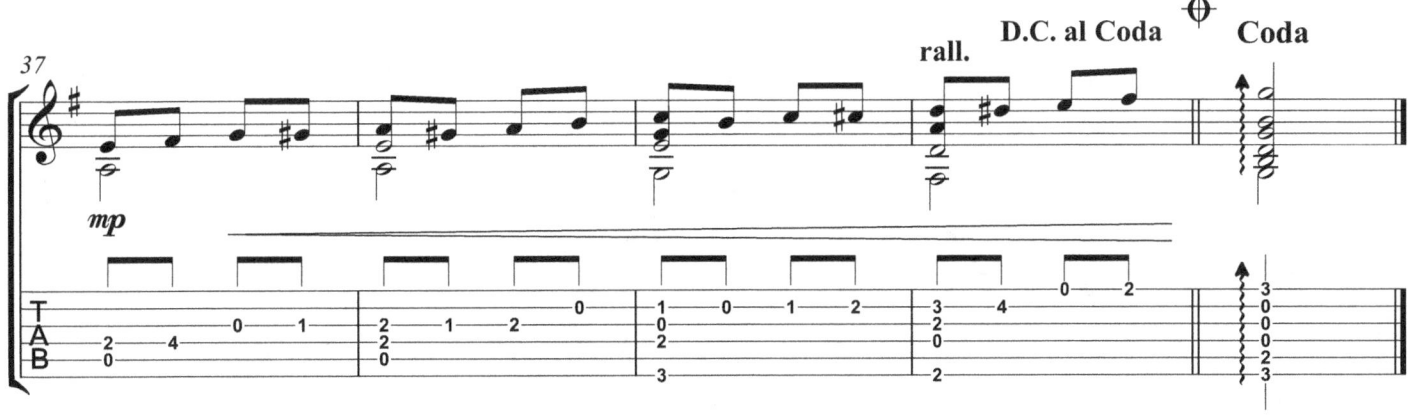

I Vow To Thee My Country

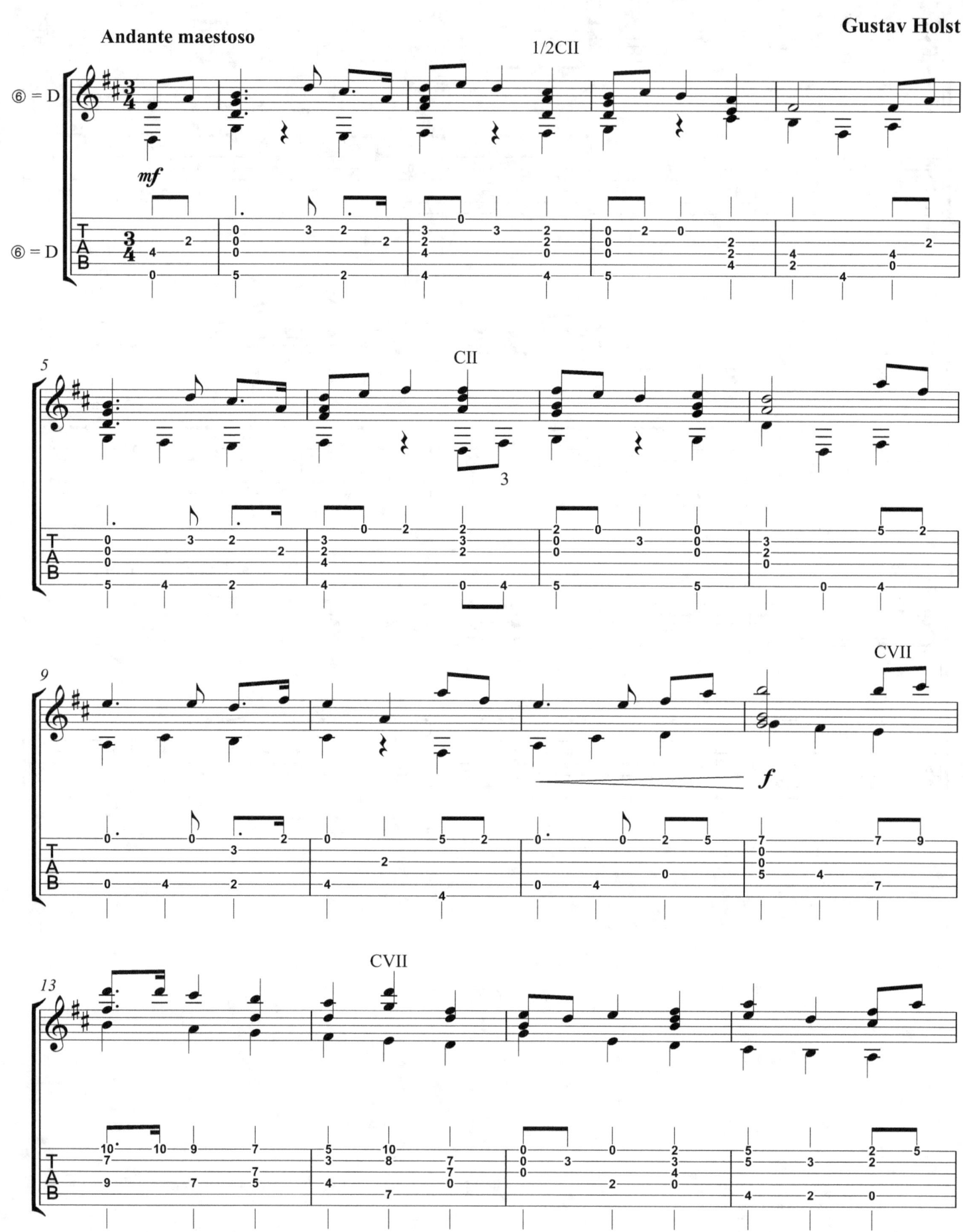

Gustav Holst

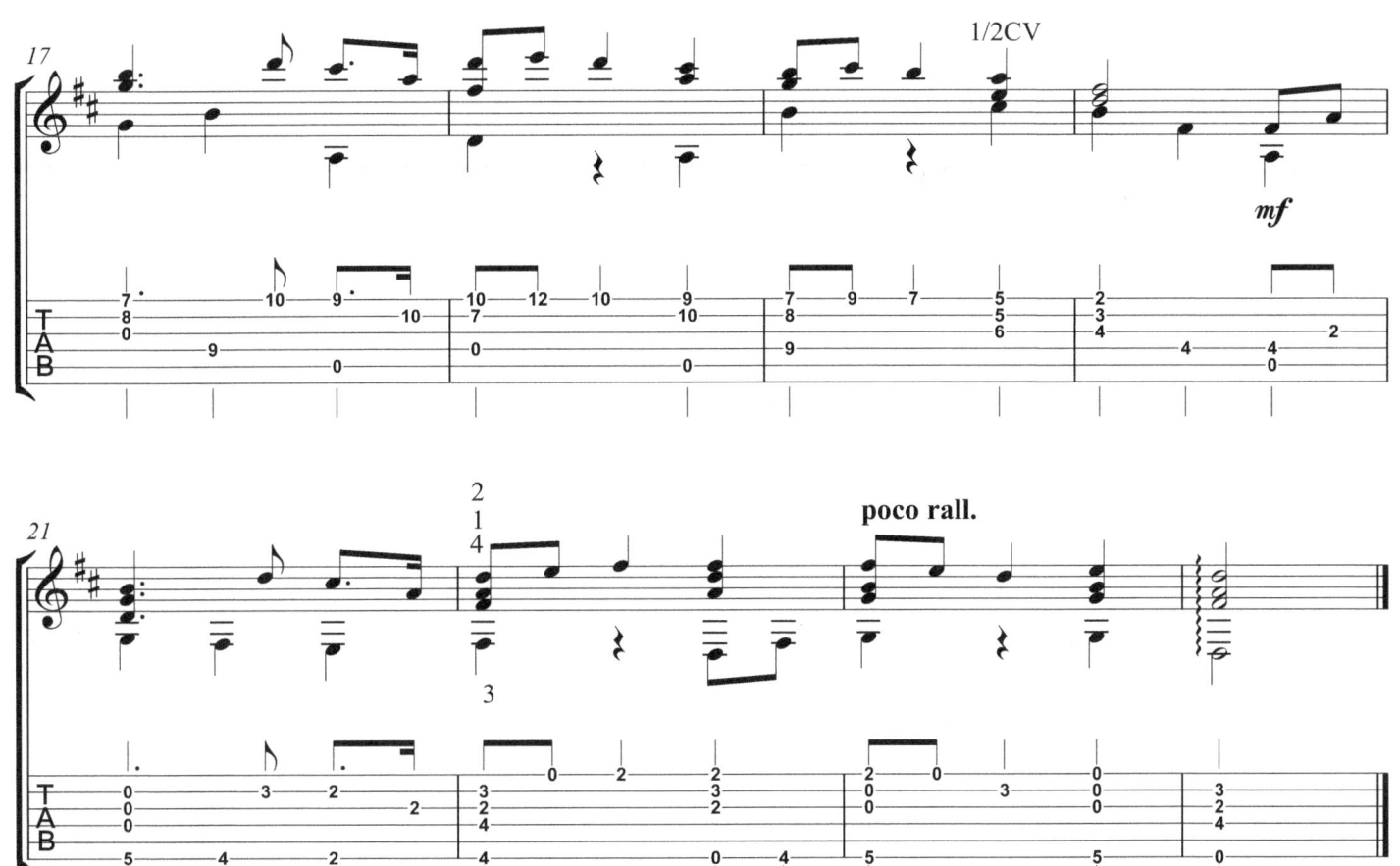

Waltz From Coppelia

Leo Delibes

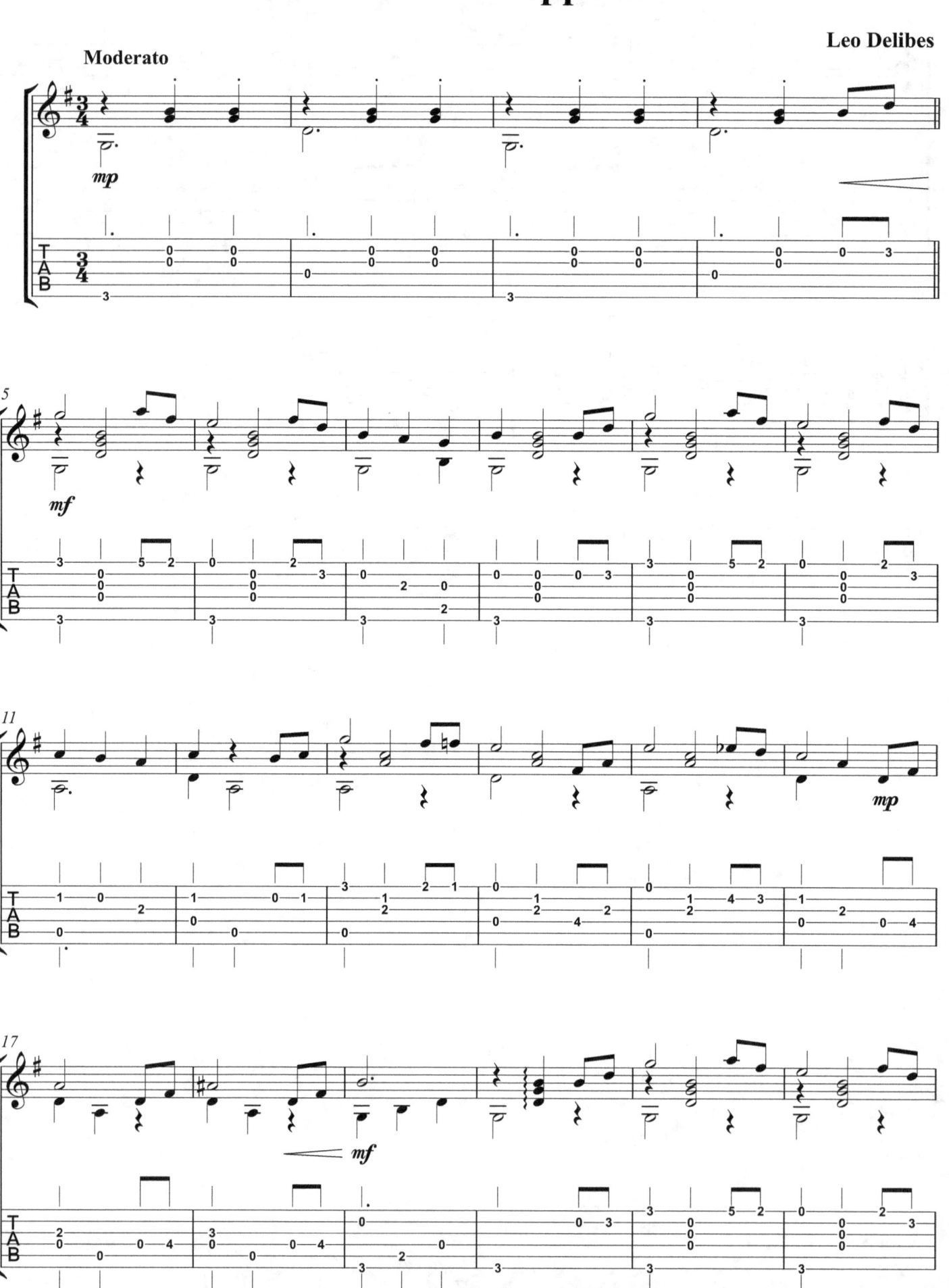

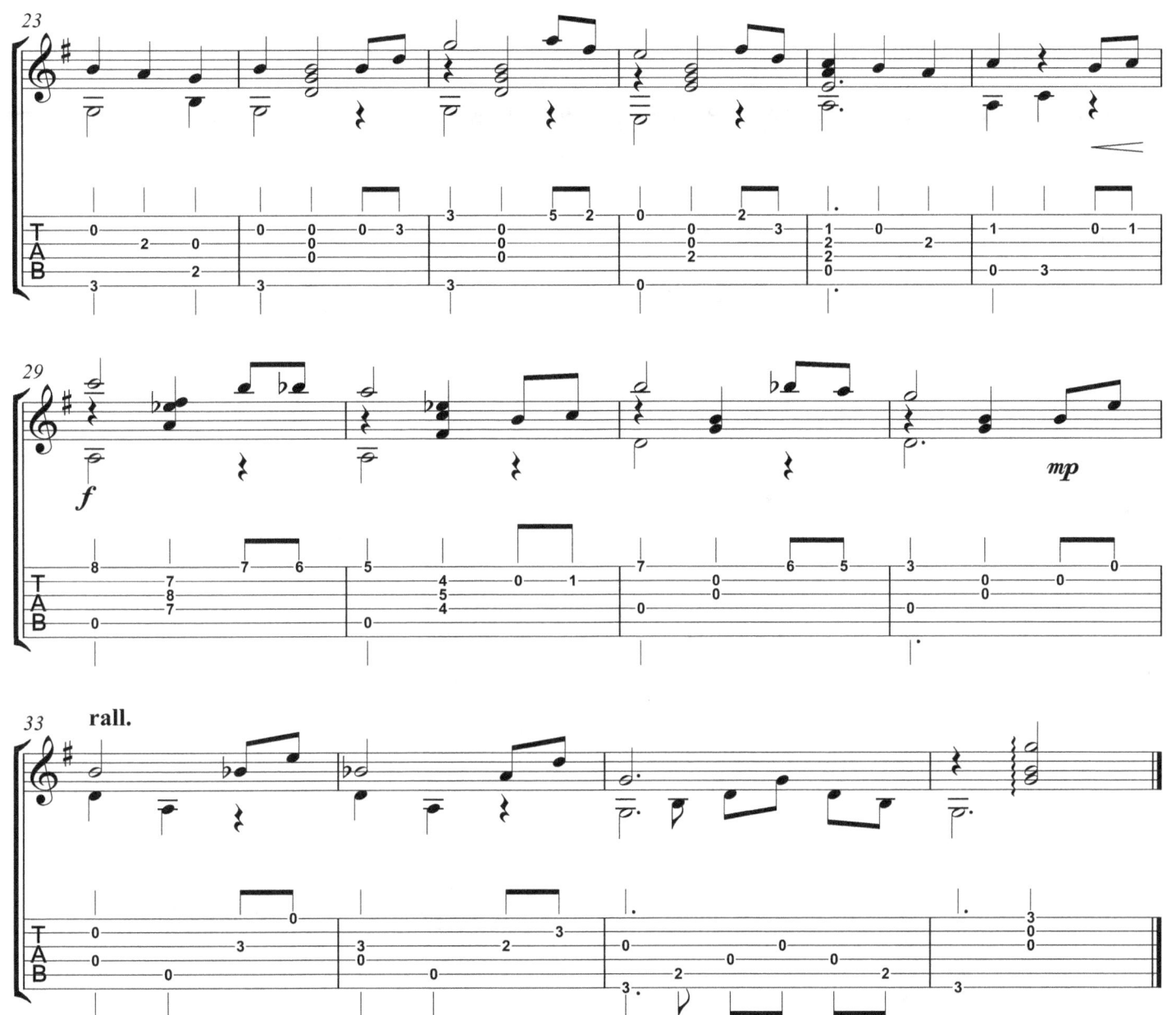

Waltz From Swan Lake

Pyotr Tchaikovsky

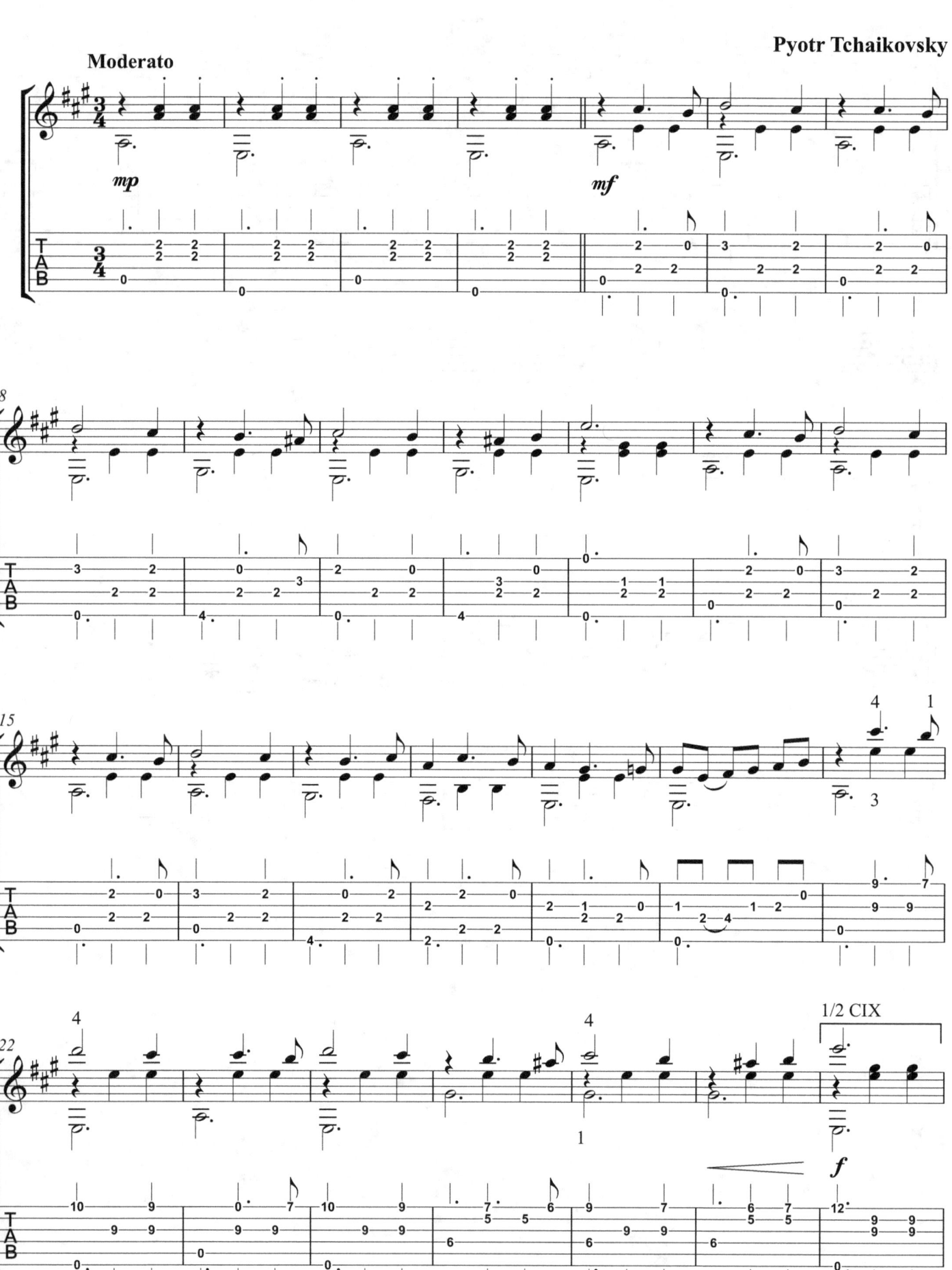

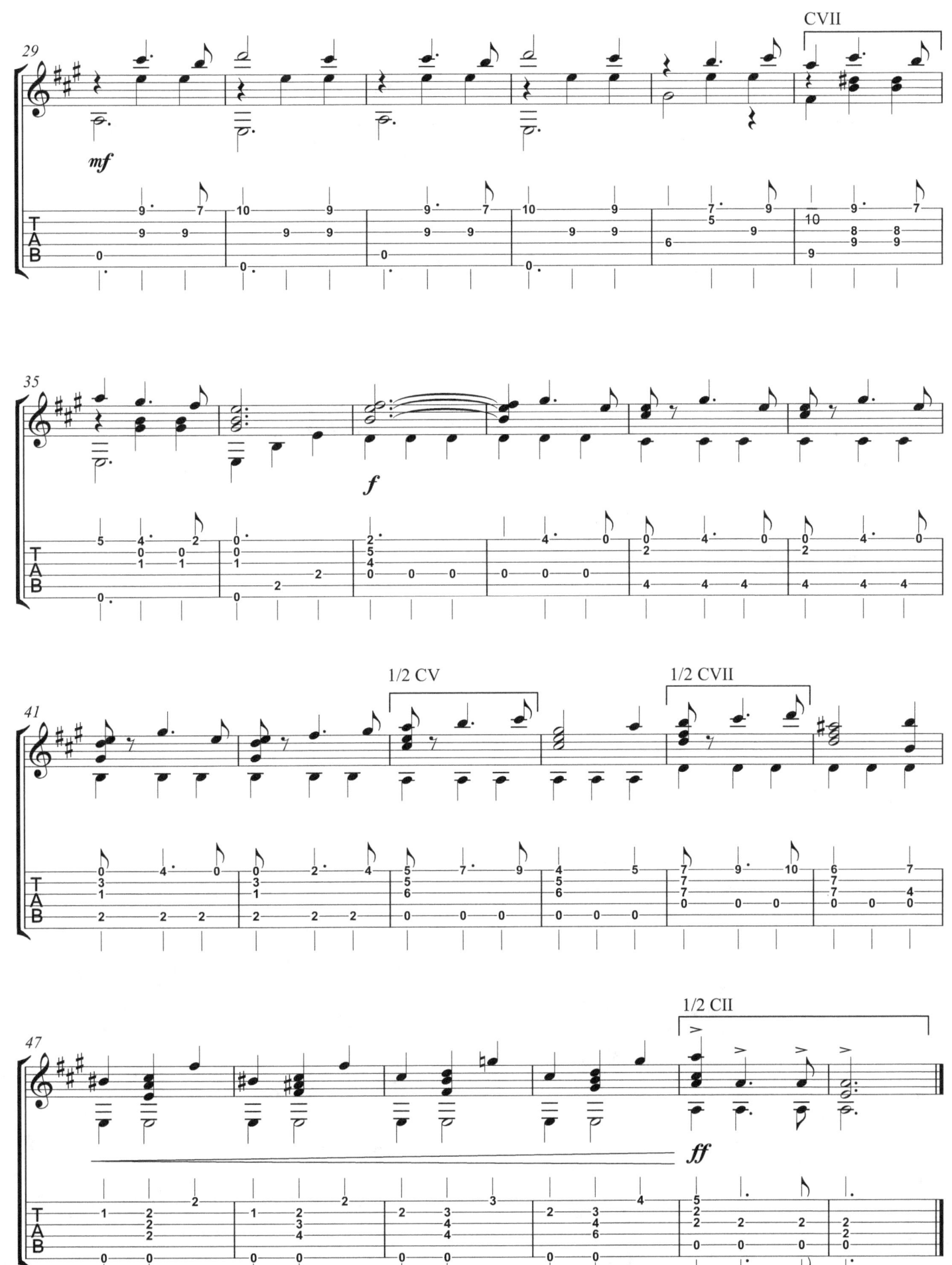

Also Available:

The Robert Burns Songbooks Vols. 1 and 2.

Arranged for classical/ fingerstyle guitar and voice.

Including:

Auld Lang Syne; Ae Fond Kiss; Ye Banks and Braes; My Love Is Like A Red, Red Rose; Ye Jacobites; There Was A Lad Was Born In Kyle; To Mary In Heaven; Mary Morison and many other favourites.

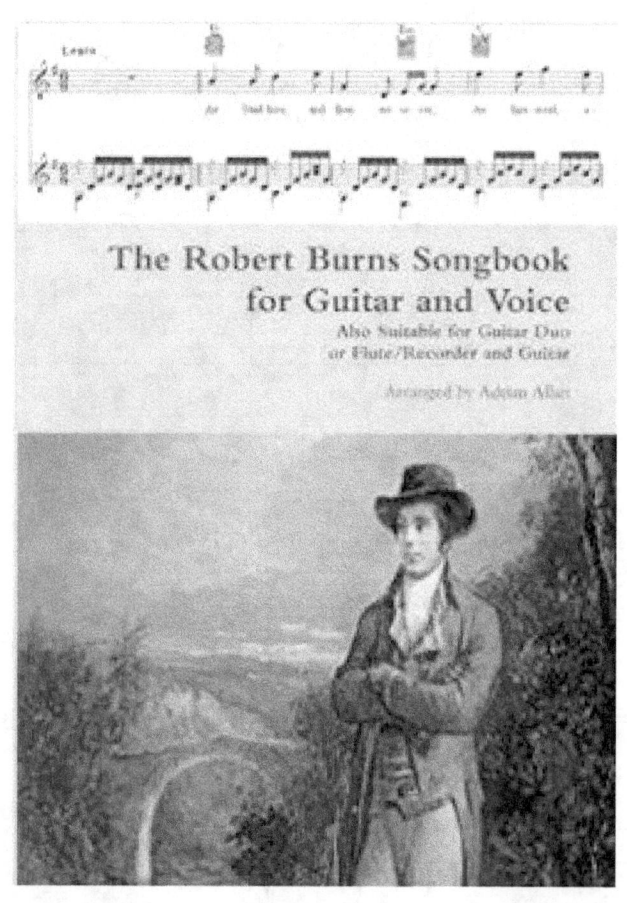

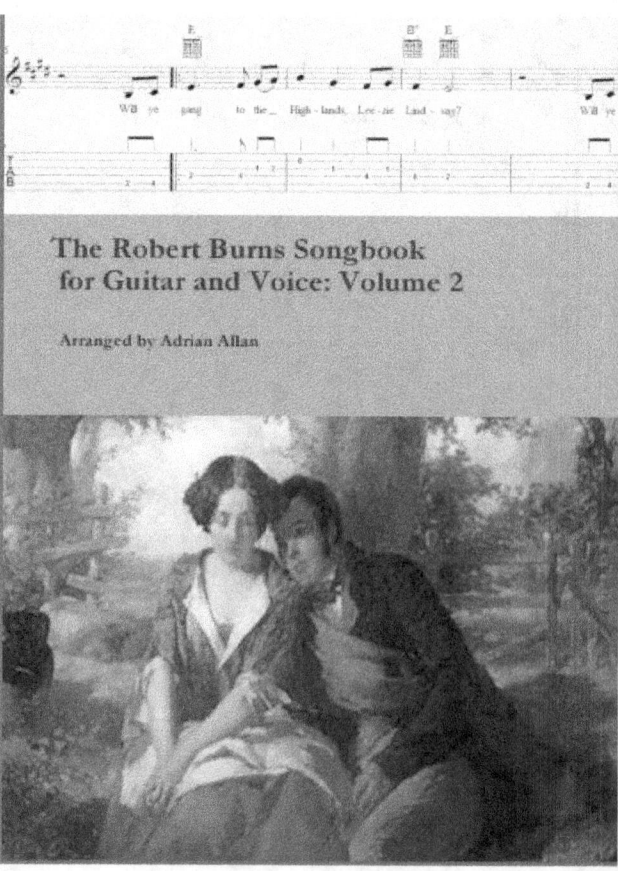

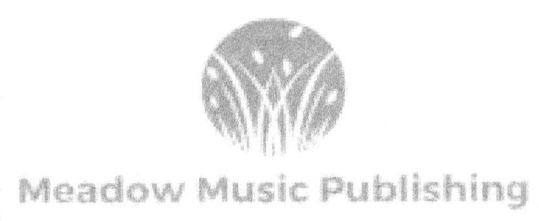
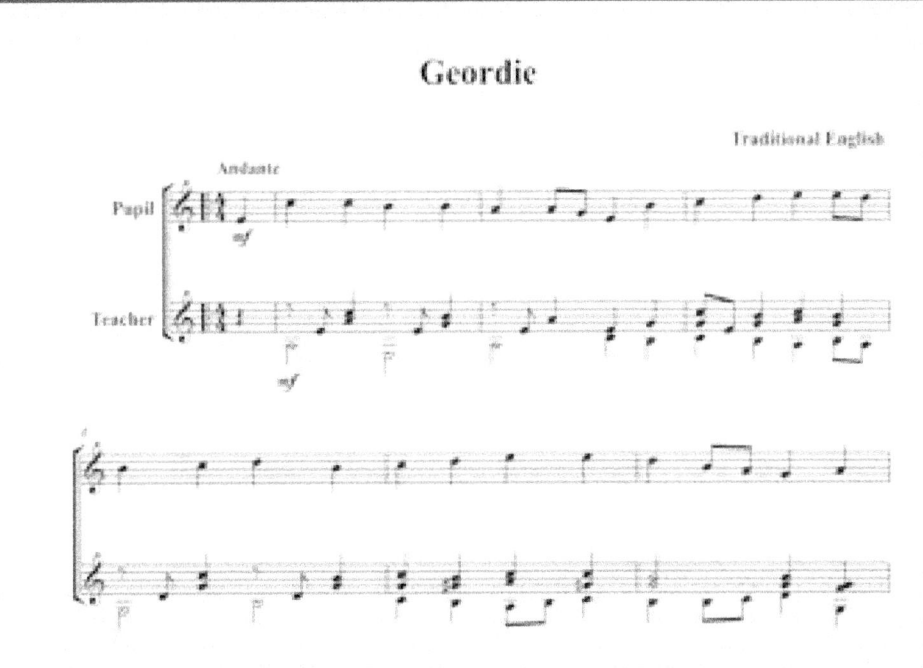
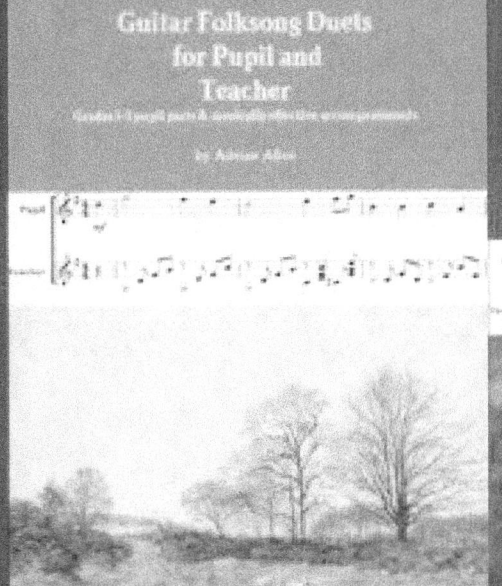

www.ingramcontent.com/pod-product-compliance
Lightning Source LLC
Chambersburg PA
CBHW081305180526
45170CB00007B/2579